D0396634

A PLACE TO PRAY

A PLACE TO PRAY

Reflections on the Lord's Prayer

ROBERTA C. BONDI

ABINGDON PRESS
Nashville

A PLACE TO PRAY: REFLECTIONS ON THE LORD'S PRAYER

Copyright © 1998 by Abingdon Press

This book is printed on recycled, acid-free, elemental-chlorine–free paper.

Book design by J. S. Lofbomm

Library of Congress Cataloging-in-Publication Data

Bondi, Roberta C.
    A place to pray : reflections on the Lord's prayer / Roberta C. Bondi.
      p. cm.
    Includes bibliographical references.
    ISBN 0-687-02574-5 (alk. paper)
    1. Lord's prayer—Meditations. I. Title.
BV230.B635   1998
226.9'606—dc21

98-35200
CIP

Scripture quotations, unless otherwise indicated, are from the New Revised Standard Version Bible, copyright © 1989, by the Division of Christian Education of the National Council of the Churches of Christ in the United States of America.

98 99 00 01 02 03 04 05 06 07—10 9 8 7 6 5 4 3 2 1

MANUFACTURED IN THE UNITED STATES OF AMERICA

TO MELISSA

PREFACE

"Our-Father-who-art-in-heaven, hallowed-be-thy-name, thy-kingdom-come, thy-will-be-done-on-earth-as-it-is-in-heaven." After "now I lay me down to sleep," this was the first grown-up prayer I ever learned to pray, and I imagine it was for a large number of the readers of this book, too. When I was a pig-tailed six-year-old still in knitted yellow pajamas with the feet in them, my mother taught me its words as a bedtime prayer. Apart from "power" and "bread," which I had always understood, and "kingdom," which I had learned about through reading fairy tales, I had very little sense of what I might be praying about.

Even as an adult I used to have problems with it. I may have studied Jesus' prayer for its original context and its meaning in that ancient context. I may have worked hard to learn how it has been interpreted theologically through the Christian centuries. I was certainly accustomed to praying it in public worship. I often heard myself reciting the words to it after I'd gone to bed for the night. In spite of everything, however, I rarely found myself paying attention to the way in which the meaning of what I was praying intersected with my own experience of God, myself, and other people.

Exactly how this came to change I cannot really tell you. I suspect it had a lot to do with the kind of understanding of the Christian life and prayer that I have learned from the Fathers and Mothers of the ancient Christian desert whom I study and teach. What I can say for certain, however, is this: for the last few years the Lord's Prayer has been one I cannot do without. It is not that I think about each word every time I say it; I often still pray it by rote—or perhaps I should say, with my body more than with my brain. Nevertheless, this is not always true. The Lord's Prayer has become my own, to form me, challenge me, console me, push me, anger me, sometimes even to make me laugh.

In many ways the Lord's Prayer is the most fundamental of all Christians' prayers. It was given to us by Jesus in response to the disciples' explicit request that he teach them to pray, and throughout the period of the early church, along with the creed, it was regarded as a basic catechetical text. For so many of us in our own period, however, praying this prayer is fraught with difficulties. Apart from the problems caused by its very familiarity, some cannot get past the first-century language to pray it in the present. Some cannot separate it from oppressive childhood experience. Others struggle in themselves against painful images of God and power which the language of the prayer evokes for them. Others, still, are simply bored.

It is my contention in this book, however, that Christians are called to love God and our neighbors as ourselves, and the Lord's Prayer, prayed honestly from the places in which we really are, is a basic tool to help us do it. This is not an exegetical book; we are blessed with a wealth of these already. Rather, what I have written in *A Place to Pray* is drawn from my own life experience, from theological reflection on what I believe the early church has to say to us, from mulling over what seem to me to be certain key passages of scripture, and from the experience of my own prayer. I have certainly not been exhaustive. In fact, you yourself might have picked out very different things to write about. I will be very happy with what I have written, however, if only it prompts and supports you in your own equivalent reflection.

Each of the following chapters is written in the form of a letter to a friend, who I like to imagine is also you, the reader. In these letters I attempt to address many of the issues that seem to make praying Jesus' prayer difficult for us today. At the same time, I try to find a way to pray the prayer as a means for healing our abilities to love God, the neighbor, and ourselves. Writing about it has helped me. I hope most sincerely that in the reading of it you will find some help, too.

So many people have supported and helped me with this project. Amy Aitken, Pam Couture, Tere Canzoneri, Marian Dolan, Carl Hall, Bill

Mallard, John Mogabgab, Bobbi Patterson, Don Saliers, and my sisters at St. Benedict's in St. Joseph, Minnesota, as well as my many students at Candler School of Theology in Atlanta.

Caroline Bynum, as usual, was a pillar of the earth, without whose encouragement I could hardly imagine myself working. Maggie Kulyk listened to everything in advance, read it, and then criticized it with intelligent sensitivity, and for all of this I am very grateful.

I especially thank three other people: my dear Melissa, who both gave me permission to write about her cancer and our friendship and who taught me so very much about living as a human being; Richard, my companion and husband; and of course, Ulrike Guthrie, my kindhearted, always competent editor at Abingdon Press.

CHAPTER ONE

My dear friend,

I was so glad to receive your letter, though I am sorry that the occasion of it is the anguish you feel at the dispute going on in your congregation over the use of the Lord's Prayer. As you describe the difficulties, one group of people object to praying it because they believe that both in its use of father language for God and in its use of language of kingdom and kingship, it is supporting the rightness of patriarchal forms of dominance and authority. Being aware of the way all of us are shaped unconsciously by the language we use, they are concerned about the long-term psychological and social effects of what seem to them to be the necessarily oppressive images carried in the words of this prayer.

The second group in your church is outraged by the objections of the first. We all have to pray this prayer, they say, whether we want to or not, because Jesus commands us to do it. God does not care how we feel about it. Our job as Christians is "to be obedient" and faithful to the tradition, not to get entangled in soul-searching and the sort of psychological concerns that they believe are destroying the church and the rest of modern society with it.

I'm sorry you are so confused and exhausted by the acrimony of the whole debate, and I regret that you can't just walk away from all this as though none of it matters. You asked me in your letter, first, how I would reply theologically and from the tradition to the objections of the warring groups in your church. Second, you wanted me to tell you how I personally pray the opening phrase of this prayer that is causing so much trouble in your church.

My friend, as you so well know, the troubles in your congregation are hardly specific to you alone; these vital issues concerning the nature of God, power, and community are being debated in all sorts of places. I am glad to try to think through your questions as best I can, therefore, because they are important for all of us. The Lord's Prayer has been infinitely significant in the lives of Christians like us over the centuries, and I could hardly bear to see us give it up. In the period of the early church the Lord's Prayer was considered to be so precious that nobody was even allowed to learn it until the very end of the three-year training period before being baptized. For Cyprian's North African community of the third century, it was the prayer that prepared them, both individually and collectively, for martyrdom. Even after the period of martyrdom was over, the Lord's Prayer continued to serve to train Christians for love in their distinctive manner of life. But let me stop lecturing on the importance of the prayer in the early church and turn to your questions.

Before I begin, however, I need to say something about the manner in which I want to answer your first question. You have asked me how I would respond "theologically and from the tradition" to the questions that have come up in your congregation. Knowing you for the length of time I have, I am afraid that what you want from me is what you generally tend to think of as "a real theological answer"—one, that is, that will cover every situation, that is rational and objective, and that is certainly free of the emotion and particularity that characterize the debate in your church.

I agree that your congregation—and we, too—certainly need theological reflection on these issues. This is one situation, however, where I disagree with your assumption that any serious theological thinking, all real theology, must always have this abstract character. In fact, having spent the last thirty years studying and teaching the practice-oriented theological tradition of early monasticism, I have come to believe that the kind of theological thinking we need to reclaim now is reflection that in the most practical and concrete way furthers the goal of the Christian life. As Jesus declares it in Mark, this goal is summed up like this: "you shall love the Lord your God with all your heart, and with all your soul, and with all your mind, and with all your strength . . . [and] you shall love your neighbor as yourself."

As I have learned so well from the fourth-, fifth-, and sixth-century traditions of the desert Fathers and Mothers, as well as from my own experience, theology that furthers the communal and personal Christian work that produces love can never be primarily abstract. It is not abstraction, after all, that moves the heart, that draws us to become in God what we are called to be, or gives us the tools that help us fulfill our calling. It is, rather, the kind of theological reflection that is a form of prayer: one in which, in the presence of God, we bring the whole of who we are, and what we have actually experienced—emotionally, bodily, rationally—into truthful conversation with scripture and the tradition. This is why I am convinced that there is no more serious, no more real and, paradoxically, no more traditional theology than this. But let me get on with answering your questions and I hope you will be able to see what I mean.

To begin. Of course, the women and men who are objecting to the use of the Lord's Prayer are right when they point out that the language and content of the prayer, too, are making political statements about power, authority, and social order that are intended to shape social relationships as well as our relationship with God at a very deep level. If we look at the rest of what Jesus says in the Gospels, it seems clear that this is just what Jesus intended.

They are also undeniably correct in their claims that the church over the centuries has used male, and particularly father, language for God, coupled with language about God's ruling authority, to dominate and oppress women (and men and children, too) in the name of God. Those who object to such oppression are doing exactly what they ought to be doing in bringing their own insight and personal experience up against what they believe the prayer is teaching, and challenging the prayer itself.

I differ with these folks, however, at the point where they give up on the prayer and refuse to fight for it. For reasons I don't fully understand, they are willing to accept a status quo reading of Jesus rather than trusting that, because God intends our life and not our death, Jesus couldn't possibly have intended to make the political statement they think Jesus is making. As a result, they neither allow this prayer to challenge what is most oppressive in the church and larger culture nor do they make use of it to begin to heal all the oppressed and suffering parts of themselves as individuals.

It is true that the prayer uses kingdom language to talk about God's governance of the world, but it seems to me to be of enormous significance that in his very use of it, Jesus subverts every ordinary notion of kings and kingship we might have. Not just the idea of rulership and rulers, either. Did I ever warn you never to invite Jesus to come to your church to speak on family values? The teenagers will love him, but the parents will be desperate! Whatever else we can say about Jesus, one thing was certain: both in his understanding of the way God governs the world and in his vision of the way human beings are to relate to one another in God's presence Jesus was radical in a way the most radical of us can never hope to be.

Jesus never told women, or men either, much less poor or oppressed people, to knuckle under and accept the status quo as God's powerful "will" for them, nor does Jesus describe God as an ordinary benevolently just ruler. On the contrary, he teaches that the folk who will have the highest place in a society of God's ordering are not the rich and successful or even the good and the religious: they are the poor, the widows and orphans, the not-so-religious, and those who are social outcasts because of the unsavoriness of their jobs. Telling his listeners in the Gospels to abandon the idea that the world as they know it has a cosmic rightness to it, he challenges them, and us, to take the risks necessary to live in this oppression-free, upside-down world right now.

As I read it, Jesus' teaching about God's fatherhood is just as subversive. I challenge anybody to find a place where Jesus uses God's fatherhood to shore up human male authority, including the authority of our own fathers. Indeed, he teaches the very opposite. "Call no one father save God alone,"[1] as I read it, says exactly the sort of things as parables like the workers in the vineyard, the good Samaritan, and even the Beatitudes. What we hold as most sacred and inviolable often has nothing to do with God's desired order. Knowing of God's extravagant generosity, do we actually think that God likes the idea that no one should get paid more than they strictly earned? Are we truly convinced, metaphorically speaking, that God regards Samaritans as unclean—that is, that God supports us in our racial, class, gender, religious, and national prejudices? In the same way, do we really believe that the God who sent us Jesus to free us from all that binds us and makes us unable to love, really desires that any of us should knuckle under and accept as "the will of God" anything that breaks our spirits or fills us with resentment or makes us think of ourselves as being intrinsically of less worth than others whether in the family, the churches, or our own society? Whatever God's fatherhood—and motherhood, creatorship, friendship, and servanthood in Jesus, too—is about, it is certainly not about this.

For understanding how God actually does act as Father toward us, no passage in scripture gives me quite so much help as an exchange recounted in the Gospel of John which Jesus had with Philip.[2] The conversation between them actually occurs in the context of a larger speech in which Jesus is trying to prepare his disciples for his death. Jesus begins by telling them that he is going to his Father's house in order to get a place ready for them. The disciples don't want to buy this for a minute. They are confused and frightened, and Thomas complains at once, "But we don't even know how to get to this house!"

Philip's questions pick up where Thomas lets off. "Who are you talking about?" he asks. "Just show us this Father and we will be quiet."

"Look," says Jesus in answer, paraphrased a bit, "look, dummy, after

---

1. Matthew 23:9. Please notice that the context in which this saying is preserved makes it very clear that what Jesus is about here is not the shoring up of the authority of God at the expense of "puny" human beings; it is the dismantling of the everyday structures of authority and respect in order to allow us to stand next to one another in a radical equality of love.

2. John 14:8.

all this time, do you still not know that if you've seen me, you have seen the Father already?"

As I read this passage, Jesus is telling us, too, that if we've seen Jesus, then we've certainly seen Jesus' own understanding of the Father in the way in which Jesus is and acts with the people around him. I know that reading this passage in John in this way raises its own problems. What, for example, are we to do with the anti-Semitism put in Jesus' mouth in the preceding chapters? Still, it means something very important to me that he spends significant time with his female friends Mary and Martha, not so much being waited on as in the exercise of real and mutual friendship. As far as I can tell, Jesus is never authoritarian, disrespectful, or bullying of these women, and he never tells them, as a large portion of the rest of their own society would have told them, to be quiet, tend to their chores, and do what their brother Lazarus wishes of them.

Of course, my friend, none of this touches your first group of people's objections that however radical Jesus' own notion of God's fatherhood, in our modern culture both in individual experience and in the context of our larger structures, including the structures of our churches, father language has, indeed, formed us and continues to form us in oppressive ways. So what are we going to do with it? Ought we to abandon it entirely?

I think not. After all, we all have or have had fathers, and many of us are fathers or have sons who will grow up to be fathers. Why should we accept that formation if these destructive images of fatherhood are inevitable? What are we doing to ourselves and our own family relationships, not to mention to our little boys and their future partners, when we suggest that maleness itself is somehow or another normatively suspect?

What we do need to do, I am convinced, is to work every day, verbally as well as by modeling with our behavior, the radical notion of God's fatherhood, and by implication, radical human fatherhood, which Jesus seems to me to teach. Will it do any good?

Let me tell you what happened one time at our house when Benjamin was sixteen. Our congregation was suffering at that time under—and it really felt "under"—the new leadership of a recent seminary graduate (he would never have made it through our seminary, I'm glad to say!) who once explained his understanding of his own role among us by using the analogy of a general in an army of privates. Richard and I were discussing the consequences of all this with anger and anguish at the family dinner table one night, as we had been doing a lot lately, while Benjamin sat there looking at his plate in bored, "not this again," teenaged silence.

Though our conversation went over the same old ground we'd been plowing for two months, that evening Richard had some stories of new high-handed acts which this time caught and outraged Benjamin's ear and moral sense. Benjamin began to fidget, rocking in his chair and mashing down his peas with the back of his fork.

"Mama," he blurted out at last, interrupting Richard in midsentence. "What's wrong with that man? Hasn't he learned that that isn't the way a minister is supposed to act? Everybody knows that God wants the minister to relate to the people in the congregation the same way the three members of the Trinity relate to each other!"

Both of us looked at Benjamin with astonishment. Our son had just clearly demonstrated a sound knowledge of trinitarian theology we had had no idea he possessed. By osmosis he had learned at church and at home that the members of the Trinity are, as we say, co-equal with each other, none above the others in power or authority. He knew why, too, in this context, it was important. The relationships of equality within the Trinity are to be our model both for human relationships within the body of Christ in general, and for leadership in particular.

But does this mean that I think everyone at church ought to address God as Father whether they want to or not? I absolutely do not. I believe we need to give people (and ourselves) plenty of room to talk about and wrestle with father language and father issues, and to accept that many people's experience is such that it has become impossible for them ever to relate to God as Father in a way that does not harm them. I have a friend my own age who is an incest survivor; I can't imagine that he ever will be able to pray to God as Father, or Mother, either, for that matter, and I feel quite certain that that is more than fine with God. There are plenty of ways to relate to God, and many names, I should hope, that we are already using in worship in addition to the name Father, that he and people like him can draw on for prayer.

Now, having told you how I would answer the objections of the first of the two warring groups of people in your congregation, let me turn to the issues of those on the other side. These are the folks who hate what they call the "psychological approach" to such questions around prayer as the ones we've been discussing, and insist, instead, on praying the Lord's Prayer because "God said it; I believe it; that settles it."

My friend, we might as well concede to them from the beginning the fact that Jesus gave his followers the Lord's Prayer with the expectation that they pray it. Presumably Jesus didn't teach his disciples the prayer just because he liked to hear himself talk. On the other hand, it is extremely important to notice that Jesus gave them this prayer not as a command—"pray this way, or else"—but, if we can trust the Gospel of Luke,[3] as a gift, as the answer to a request the disciples thought up themselves, namely, that he teach them how to pray.

To begin, as I just said with respect to God's fatherhood, we must notice that while Jesus frequently describes and challenges us in what we are called to in our life in God, he is not at all, in fact, either in the habit of laying down the law for those who would follow him, or telling people to do what he says without thinking or questioning it. Indeed, it would be easy to argue, on the contrary, that Jesus uses parables in the way he does precisely in order to get his listeners to ask questions to help them to think deeply about God, their neighbors, and themselves in unsettling new ways.

Now to what this group in your congregation rather sneeringly calls the "psychological approach" to Christianity. As I understand them, by "the psychological approach" they mean, first, taking seriously and discussing our own experience with other Christians, especially where it seems to contradict the tradition, and second, wrestling with the way the norms and

---

3. Luke 11:1 ff.

expectations of the larger culture shape us interiorly and thereby keep us from being the loving people God calls us to be.

Let there be no mistake: If this is what they mean by "the psychological approach," I am in favor of it. In fact, I want to state again clearly that I, as well as many who consider themselves to be very "traditional" Christians from the time of the early church onward, believe that the goal and the point of the Christian life Jesus summons us to is nothing more or less than the love of God, which we are to exercise with all our hearts, strength, minds, and soul, and the love of our neighbor as ourselves. To put it in other terms, I think that what Jesus is asking of us is a total transformation into the love of God and neighbor of our entire persons, interior and exterior, public and private, social and personal, hearts, minds, strength, and souls.

But Jesus did not just command us to love in this radical way and then expect us to be able to grit our teeth and do it all at once by an exercise of massive, blind obedience that bypasses interior reflection and work. In fact, just the opposite. The parables of the workers in the vineyard, the prodigal son, the good Samaritan, and the unforgiving servant, for example, all seem to me to have been intended to help his listeners radically open their hearts to a deep examination of their internal and external family experience, perceptions, motives, desires, and values, as well as of the religious, social, and personal expectations which govern them. In this way, Jesus pushes his listeners and us, too, longer and harder than the most aggressive and probing modern therapist.

As for the charge that such a "psychological approach" is not traditional, though they go about their work in different ways from us, it is indeed the approach of the wonderful ancient teachers of the early church from the fourth through the sixth centuries on which I work.

Did I ever tell you this story from the *Sayings of the Fathers* which illustrates my point?[4] Once there was a foreign anchorite who made a long and tiring trip to the Egyptian desert to look for the great Abba

---

4. Poemen 8, *The Sayings of the Desert Fathers,* English trans. Benedicta Ward (London and Oxford: Mowbray, 1981), p.167.

Poemen to listen to his wisdom and learn from him. The visitor was so happy when he finally found Poemen that as soon as he went through the door of his house he began "to speak," as the text says, "of the Scriptures, of spiritual and heavenly things."

Poemen, however, who was normally a friendly man, unexpectedly refused to hold up his end of the conversation or otherwise answer him. The poor bruised visitor finally left to look for the brother who had originally introduced him to Poemen to see if he could discover why Poemen wouldn't talk to him.

This brother then went and asked Poemen directly why he had ignored the famous holy man from so far away. Poemen's reply was unequivocal: "He is great and speaks of heavenly things and I am lowly and speak of earthly things. If he had spoken of the passions of the soul, I should have replied, but he speaks to me of spiritual things and I know nothing about that."

Upon receiving the brother's report, the visitor understood his mistake. For Abba Poemen, lofty spiritual talk about the demands of God and even about scripture is only a distraction from the real business of the Christian life, which is the transformation and healing of whatever it is that destroys our ability to love God with all our hearts, souls, strength, and mind, and our neighbors as ourselves. These are what the ancient teachers and theologians called the passions,[5] exactly those deep, long-term attitudes of heart, mind, feeling, and perception, like anger, unforgivingness, ingratitude, inattentiveness, envy, judgmentalism, self-righteousness, and greed, that Jesus addresses in the Gospels.

Having learned this lesson, the visitor went back to Poemen and tried again, saying, "What should I do, Abba, for the passions of the soul master me?" This time, the abba received him happily and talked to him about

---

5. For an ancient description and classification of the passions see "The Praktikos" in *Evagrius Pontikos: The Praktikos, Centuries on Prayer*, trans. John Eudes Bamberger, O.C.S.O. (Spenser, Mass.: Cistercian Publications, 1970). For a modern discussion see "The Passions" in my *To Love as God Loves: Conversations with the Early Church* (Minneapolis: Augsburg/ Fortress, 1987). For why I believe it is important that we recover this tradition of understanding the passions, see chapter 1 of my *In Ordinary Time: Healing the Wounds of the Heart* (Nashville: Abingdon Press, 1996).

the actual stuff of their lives, which I imagine included such topics as the specific, long-term ways they were each combating their perfectionism, their impatience, their consumerism, their judgmentalism, their smoldering angers, and their need to have others' approval of them.

This tradition which stresses the importance of such introspective work is one that I find entirely useful in our own times, usually more useful, in fact, than the kind of doctrinal discussions that simply end in pronouncements. However much we might like to tell ourselves otherwise, there just isn't any way we can love one another or God as God really is if we can't even see God or our actual neighbors because of our various combinations of misperceptions, self-deceptions, and psychological and spiritual injuries to the image of God in us.

With respect to the place of this work in our common worship, it is my experience that worship not only depends upon us doing the interior work and seeking the healing we need to be able to hear what God asks of us and respond to it, real worship itself forms us into who we are individually and as the people of God. This formation, whether we are aware of it or not, takes place as we are attentive to scripture, as we hear and preach sermons, as we participate in intercessory prayers, and as we share together in the Lord's Supper.

But, my friend, you did not only ask me to help you think about and respond to the issues of the folks in your church: you also wanted me to tell you a little about why and how I pray this part of the Lord's Prayer myself.

As for the why, I pray the whole of the prayer, first, as a basic and deliberate part of my own ongoing formation as a Christian in the ways of love. I need it; it is one of the major places I can bring for healing both my short-term convictions, feelings, confusions, prejudices, and actions, and my whole long-term autobiographical self, including personal and cultural memories of my childhood and adult experiences and expectations that have formed me and fight in me still against the patterns of love.

At the same time, in the context of this daily self-examination I also need this prayer as a guide and corrective to my intercessory prayer. I need it to help me remember whom to pray for, and I need it for something else, besides. I don't know about you, but I somehow learned in my growing-up years that I must set aside my own "selfish" needs and desires in order to pray for other people. As a result, I have to keep learning over and over that there is a fundamental connection between how much actual compassion and empathy I can feel for the needs of others and my ability to accept that what I need is valid, too. What does it say that I really think about other people's needs if I consider it somehow morally superior for me to "rise above" my own? I must pray this prayer, therefore, for myself, not only to teach me what to pray for the people with whom I share my life and my world, but to train me in an ever-growing vulnerability and empathy for them as well.

As for the mechanics of how I pray this prayer, it is probably obvious to you by now that when I am praying alone I don't go straight through it as we recite it in church. Instead, I use it as a guide for my prayer. I begin by speaking the words of the first phrase. Then I meditate briefly, or at length if I need to, on what I believe that part of the prayer is guiding me toward. Finally, in a short sentence or two I rephrase what I am asking God for on that particular day. Needless to say, what I ask for varies considerably depending on what is going on in both my interior and my exterior life.

But let me stop explaining and simply show you what I mean by going through the first words of the Lord's Prayer for you as I have sometimes prayed it in the past and as I actually pray it each day now.

I begin each morning with the phrase that as often as not is now the most important part of my prayer: *"Our Father in heaven."*

You will probably not be surprised to know that for many years the word in this phrase that I responded to the fastest was "Father," and my response was one of pain and anger.[6] Part of my difficulty lay, as it does for the people in your congregation, with my inability to escape the way

---

6. For a fuller discussion of what I consider to be the problems around the language of God's Fatherhood and the solutions to those problems, see chapter 1 of my *Memories of God: Theological Reflections on a Life* (Nashville: Abingdon Press, 1995).

God's fatherhood had been used to support a status quo in the church and in the culture that hurts women and had hurt me.

In addition, in terms of my own particular experience, I had also grown up in the forties and fifties with a loving but authoritarian, perfectionistic father who left the family when I was eleven. Like many other people, having transferred to God the Father all the pain I felt around my human father, I simply couldn't get past the father language of the prayer to reach God.

Though I was aware of all this at the time, I was hurting so much and so mistrustful of God that I simply couldn't face trying to work through these issues in my prayer. During this period, I found when I prayed that it helped me, as it has helped so many other people I have spoken with, to substitute a name, like Mother or Friend, that actually would allow me to approach God rather than turn me away.

A long time passed after that in which through my everyday prayer I actually began to learn something firsthand about the trustworthiness of the God I couldn't yet address as Father. Then, several things happened that allowed me to become desperate enough as well as brave and trusting enough to do the work of prayer I needed to do around the issue of calling God "Father." I pored over scripture for help, and in God's presence I began to be able to understand in my own heart what I told you a few pages ago about the radical implications I heard in Jesus' words when he said to Philip, "The one who has seen me has seen the Father."

As I continued to bring my own past and present experience into painful, direct conversation with God through the help of this and other passages of scripture, I found myself increasingly freed from my secret belief that the way my father had been with me as a child was somehow a normative description not just of God but of the power men have a right to exercise over women in the world.

But remember, I said that I pray the Lord's Prayer for formation in love of God and neighbor together, so you will not be surprised to hear that learning to understand God's fatherhood in new ways also helped me significantly with my pain over my human father. Once having stopped confusing my father with God, I was able to forgive my father for his failures toward me and let my father simply be who he was—not God, but simply a human being with ordinary weaknesses. It was allowing my father to be no more than human, as much as anything else, that made it possible for me to experience myself as his fully adult child. Then, at last, I could be reconciled with him and learn to love him, enjoy him for the actual man he was, and care for him in a way appropriate to him.

Do you know, these days, when those old scars around questions of male authority itch and I begin once more to feel internally trapped by the sexism all of us still encounter, I nearly always get help at once by praying, "Our Father who art in heaven," followed immediately by, "God, I know your fatherhood is not underwriting and supporting this stuff that hurts me; rather, your fatherhood calls me into life and fills me with energy. Help me repudiate the hold these things have on me." My wounds associated with God's fatherhood are fairly well healed for the most part now, and so I don't often find myself needing to pray this way for myself, though I still must pray for other people—and the church—who are struggling with their own injuries around fallen notions of God's fatherhood.

Oddly, now the part of the phrase "our Father in heaven" that daily grips me, instead, is the seemingly much less difficult word, "our." "Our" is a tough word for me in this prayer and I'm working hard at it.

"Oh, no," my friend, I can hear you saying to yourself, "are you losing your mind? In the light of all the difficulties around praying to God the Father, what on earth could make praying the perfectly ordinary word 'our' an issue for you?"

Well, I'll start by reminding you of what we acknowledge all the time, which is that twentieth-century Protestant Americans are almost fatally individualistic in every area of our lives, including our religion. I am still a product of my own culture, Christian or not, and so I continue to fall into the trap of thinking of *my* spirituality and *my* prayer as a private matter involving nobody but myself and God.

As if this were not enough to fight against as I try to learn to love, like everybody else I also have to deal with my own temperament and the way

A Place to Pray

I have been formed by the things that happened to me both as a child and as an adult which have made me who I am. I've already mentioned that I grew up with a difficult father. One of the things that was difficult about him was that he wanted me to be "the best" at everything, and so he did what he could to make sure I thought of myself as both superior to and different from the other perfectly nice, smart children with whom I went to school. Nothing would make him madder, for example, than my request for a particular item of clothing that "everybody else" wore or for a toy "everybody else" played with, unless it was my use of the slang they spoke in.

Predictably enough, his plan to make me superior and independent backfired. Being a very shy, unpopular child who was excruciatingly aware of her faults, I found it impossible to think of myself as better than anybody. In fact, however my father wanted me to see myself, what I knew was that in most significant ways I was an outcast from childhood society.

The Baptist religion of the Kentucky relatives I visited in the summer didn't make things easier for me, either. My assumption that God the Father's demands were very like my human father's, coupled with my inability to "believe God loved me and accept Jesus as my Lord and Savior," told me that I must be an outcast in God's kingdom as I was in the kingdom of school.

Will it make sense to you now if I tell you, therefore, that when I prayed the first words of the Lord's Prayer as a child, what I said was "*our* Father who art in heaven," but what I meant was "*their* Father who art in heaven"? The god I knew was the Father of the good, deserving children who belonged in the society of other children or adults in a way I never found I could.

Even in my early adult years I couldn't escape this sense of isolation and abandonment. You know already how much guilt and hopelessness I suffered as a woman violating the status quo by going to graduate school and taking up teaching back in the sixties and seventies. It probably won't surprise you to hear, therefore, that during the whole of that time, I continued to experience God as I had as a child, not as "my Father" who supported my socially unacceptable desires and ambitions, but rather as the Father of those whom the culture considered "good."

My adult life wasn't all hard, of course, and I made some progress against my sense of being an outcast in a world I hadn't been able to live in comfortably over the years. The birth of my children, the presence of my second husband in my life, and my teaching all helped me enormously. The words of the great desert teachers I study began to give me saving help as soon as I met them. Still, even having made such progress, about fifteen years ago I realized I wanted to move much farther out of what had become by then a mostly interior isolation from other people and God.

I began with God. At that time, under the influence of my teachers from the early church, I began a discipline of prayer that enabled me to learn firsthand, face to face, how different God is from the rejecting, hypercritical god I had imagined. Ultimately, it was here in my daily prayer as I learned to bring my own experience into conversation with the tradition of the early monasticism I study, and with scripture, particularly the Psalms and the Gospels, that I began to know what it meant to me personally to say that God is the God of the despised, the socially outcast, and the rejected.

This was real progress. At last, I was able to pray the Lord's Prayer as my own prayer, to pray "*our* Father in heaven" and mean by these words, not "*their* Father," but "*my own* Father." It was wonderful. For the first time in my life it did not seem to me that God was on one side of the universe attending to everybody else while I was all alone on the other. God was with me. I knew God both as the safe place I could turn when I felt alone or afraid and as the one who supported me in my desire to do the work I felt called to do. When I found myself under the pressures of living and working with another real live person or persons who had hurt me or angered me, or whose expectations I felt unable to meet, or who just plain wore me out, I could withdraw into the safe space of my prayer and pray: "*my* Father in heaven," "give *me* this day *my* daily bread," "lead *me* not into temptation."

For a while, it was enough. Then the day came when I could no longer let myself forget that in this particular prayer, what Jesus teaches is not how to pray "*my* Father who is in heaven," but rather "*our* Father." Neither finding a safe space nor being supported by God is the goal of the Christian life; it is love of God, but it is love of neighbor, too.

For help in learning how to pray "*our* Father" and mean it, I began to meditate frequently on what I first read in the commentary on the Lord's Prayer by the third-century North African Cyprian:[7] at some level it doesn't matter whether I think I am praying this prayer alone or whether I consciously acknowledge my basic identity as a member of the body of Christ when I pray it. My unity with other Christians, after all, isn't something I must make happen myself. Whether I want it or not, the fact is that whenever I speak these words, "*our* Father," "give *us . . . our* daily bread," by virtue of my very baptism I am praying it as part of the people of God, and in return they are praying it with me.

Of even more help to me now, however, is a way of praying the first words of the Lord's Prayer that only came to me about a year ago.

Over a period of weeks I had been unsuccessfully struggling to forgive what I had experienced as a significant betrayal by a close friend I'll call Jane Anne. I was fairly sure she was unaware of what she had done to me, and I had no intention of trying to talk with her about it: some days I told myself that trying to discuss it would only make my feelings toward her worse; other days I wanted to believe that what I felt would go away if I just didn't pay any attention to it.

Neither strategy worked, nor were my prayers for help in forgiveness successful. Though I had days when my anger and hurt receded a little, for no apparent reason, on as many other days my pain and rage were as new and sharp as they had been in the beginning. One part of me—the

---

7. "Before all things the Teacher of peace and Master of unity is unwilling for prayer to be made singly and individually, teaching that he [or she] who prays is not to pray for himself [or herself] alone. For we do not say, *My Father Who art in heaven,* nor *Give me this day my bread. . . .* Prayer with us is public and common; and when we pray we do not pray for one but for the whole people, because we the whole people are one." Trans. by T. Herbert Bindley in *St. Cyprian on the Lord's Prayer* (London: SPCK, 1914), pp. 32-33.

smaller part in which God's grace is always calling me to truthfulness and vulnerability, however—knew that love is too valuable ever to be thrown away and that I still valued my friend. Still, the larger part of me—the old, wounded, isolated part—felt that the very ground had fallen away under my feet. All I wanted to do was simply follow my familiar patterns of safety by praying for myself and going away never to see her again.

I struggled on with my prayer, nonetheless, and one morning, feeling really hopeless, as I began to pray Jesus' prayer, I heard myself praying the opening words in a new way. "*Our* Father who art in heaven," I heard myself say and then immediately after that, "*my* Father and *the Father of Jane Anne....*"

My friend, I hardly know how to tell you what happened next. It was entirely undramatic, but all at once I realized that as I said these words, "my Father and the Father of Jane Anne," I knew I was no longer alone in a private world in which I was blinded and isolated by my own mental anguish. Rather, I found myself in the presence of God, Jane Anne beside me, in the bright and open space of God's mysterious love for the two of us. Immediately, my grief and anger began to lift. For the first time since what I'd thought of as her original betrayal, I understood that the issue I had been wrestling with was not so much my specific need to forgive Jane Anne for what she had done as it was my old need to keep my footing on what I thought of as my hard-earned place in the universe in which everybody else lived.

By speaking the words "my Father and the Father of Jane Anne" I had prayed for her and myself together. Somehow, in that moment when I was given the gift of praying "*our* Father" and really meaning it, I knew I had a place already I didn't have to fight for or defend; it was a place in the family of God to which I belonged simply because I was a human being. Finally, freed of my blinding fear, I was set loose to begin to see and love Jane Anne with empathy and compassion.

Still, there was the shadow of the original betrayal lying between us. What was I to do? In the days that followed I continued to pray for myself and Jane Anne together as I had been doing. Finally, it became clear to me that I must tell her my feelings and give her a chance to respond. The conversation wasn't easy, but it helped each of us see what had happened in a new light, to repair what had been broken, and to grow together toward the future.

What I have learned from all this for dealing with my long-term struggles to pray "our Father" and my ongoing desire to grow in love through my prayer has been enormously important to me. Each morning now, I begin to pray the Lord's Prayer by saying the words "our Father." After that, I visualize the face or faces of the people I must be with that day with whom I am angry, or whom I would avoid because they have hurt me or sap my energy or exercise internal or external destructive power over me. Then, I paraphrase the words "our Father" and repeat them as a prayer for myself and for the other person or persons together: "my Father and the Father of my student Stephen"; "my Father and the Father of the church group I am on my way to speak to"; "my Father and the Father of my uncle."

Though if I am angry enough at someone, I have to prod and push myself to pray it, I know that this is a necessary way for me to pray. Mysteriously, as it once happened with my prayer for myself and Jane Anne together, what nearly always comes along with the words of the prayer is an immediate, intimate awareness of our being equally loved members of God's family. This awareness seems to take away my own defensiveness and self-protection and lets me be more present with the other person or persons on that day in the way they—and I, too—need.

Why praying in this manner should be helpful I don't know for sure. I suspect it is connected with what Dorotheos of Gaza told the brothers of his quarreling sixth-century monastery.[8] "How can you fight this way?" he said to them in effect. "Don't you know that you should be praying instead, 'by the prayers of my brother, save me'?"

Perhaps whenever we stand before God and pray at the same time for ourselves and for someone else from whom we feel separated we are step-

---

8. *Dorotheos of Gaza: Discourses and Sayings,* trans. Eric P. Wheeler (Kalamazoo: Cistercian Publications, 1977), p. 154.

ping into a place of humility that lets us admit to ourselves that our own lives depend not only on the prayers of strangers but even on the prayers of our enemies. I don't know whether other people will be helped by such an admission, but I have come to believe that my own life is being saved in this way at this very moment.

No matter, perhaps, that I can't explain this mysterious process of learning to pray the word "our" better than I have. Whatever our capacity to explain, the healing of our ability to love is never something that we do ourselves; healing always finally comes as a gift of God.

At any rate, I'm sorry for your troubles, my friend, and I hope you are able to find something in this very long letter that will help you with the tough situation in your church. Don't give up; as you can see, I believe the conversation you are in is terribly important. Perhaps, if you aren't already doing it, you might try praying the Lord's Prayer for yourself and your congregation together in the way we have been talking about. Whether you do or not, I'll keep you in my prayers, and you keep me in yours, too.

Yours in Christ,
Roberta

CHAPTER TWO

My good friend,

I am very glad that you found what I said about the first words of the Lord's Prayer helpful. Of course, I will be glad to think with you about what you so gracefully call the next "killer phrase" in the Lord's Prayer, "hallowed be your name," and yes, I'll be happy to tell you how I pray it myself. I have certainly been pondering the whole of what Jesus passed on to us for a very long time. I know it will give me pleasure as well as help for my own prayer to be able to put a few more of these thoughts on paper.

Before I get started on "hallowed be your name," though, you asked me in your letter if it is true that I really had never thought about what it meant to pray "our" Father in heaven until quite recently. I know you are teasing me when you say that if it is the case, then I am a little slow. I'm afraid I have to admit I am, and not just about this, either. You should see the stacks of unfiled papers and unanswered letters I have in my office at school, not to mention the unironed clothes and the messy kitchen at home.

On the other hand, aren't we all slow—even you?—when it comes to discovering things in our prayer? Haven't you noticed yourself how for years you can hear the same passage of scripture or of some familiar prayer or, in my case, a saying from the *Sayings of the Fathers*, without any meaning registering on your heart at all? Then, all of a sudden, there you are in a crisis of some sort, and words pop up in your mind, probably out of context, but as clear and alive as if they had been written for this specific need of yours in the first place.

That God and the human heart work like this would be a good reason to memorize passages of scripture, prayers, and other items we might expect to be useful, except I'm not sure we would ever consciously choose the right thing to learn. Somehow, God seems to need the whole sloppy body of what we carry around with us, not just the "good parts," but the psalms we never meant to get by heart, the words of a hymn we may not even fully remember, phrases of parables, a quotation from the tradition we may not have understood, and yes, for myself, this prayer of Jesus as well.

A friend of mine who was in the hospital for months after a car accident told me how, as she lay in bed in excruciating pain recovering from, among other things, nerve damage to her upper right arm, she was frequently comforted by the words of a liturgical prayer that had always frightened her as a child. Each day as she struggled to endure what felt like blue flames burning in the skin and muscles of her damaged arm, she found herself repeating, "Save me, O God, from the fires of hell." Who, except a person you and I might judge to be fixated on sin and judgment in the worst way, would ever have memorized that particular prayer with the expectation that someday it might provide a sense of the intimately healing presence of God?

Whatever we might want to say to the contrary, I think all of this goes toward demonstrating that real prayer is a conversation with God which, as much as we might like to, we can't really script to suit ourselves. At least, we can't assign God's lines in advance, get God to recite them in our minds, and then say we've had an actual conversation, or gotten any genuinely new insight. I suppose this ought to be obvious, but somehow it isn't. For myself, I know I am often so busy telling myself what God must be saying to me in a given situation that I can't be attentive to the way God actually does frequently speak: that is, in totally unexpected words in utterly surprising places—surprising sometimes simply because the words and places are so very familiar.

But, to turn to the Lord's Prayer and the specific problems you have with praying "hallowed be your name": You say in your last letter that you can't even think about what it might mean for something, even God's name, to be "hallowed" or holy anymore without hearing in your mind what has become in our culture the familiar language of "us against them." To talk about "the sanctity" of something no longer seems to you to be about the actual holiness of God or holy things as much as it is about using God to preserve our own purity and to ratify our condemnation, hatred, or dismissal of other people or groups who disagree with us on moral issues.

I admit that I, too, have had trouble with what I have consciously called holiness a lot of my life. As a child, the very idea of God's holiness carried with it God's dangerously righteous hatred of sin, as well as the threat of God's anger, which could blaze out suddenly against even the most innocent of mistakes. How I arrived at this judgment I don't entirely know. It was partly from the revivals at Pond Fork Baptist Church, the white country church I attended in the summer when my mother and brothers and I would visit my grandparents in Union County, Kentucky. Though I remember plenty of talk about hell and God's hatred of sin, outside of stern warnings about "keeping the sabbath holy," I can't remember any explicit discussion of God's holiness. I suspect that part of my trouble came from my childhood confusion between the characteristics of my human father and my heavenly one. God surely was like my father, only even bigger, more perfectionistic, and more powerful, wasn't he?

For whatever reason I understood it in the way I did, however, my first remembered encounter with what I identified at the time as the holiness of God goes back to an event that took place in the sixth grade, when my family was living in Delaware.

As you know, Mama had been raised Southern Baptist, and though she became a Methodist in her adolescent years (probably as an act of rebellion!), while she was married to my nonreligious Yankee father, she usually simply brought us to the nearest house of worship in the Calvinist tradition. In Wilmington, where we moved from New York when I was eleven, it was a white-columned, red brick Dutch Reformed Church close to the new suburb in which we lived.

It was a beautiful building, as it stands in my memory. It was surrounded on the outside by large shade trees old enough to make the soft grass and woolly moss beneath them lumpy with their roots. Inside, the austerely aristocratic sanctuary, hung with curving brass chandeliers, was tall and full of light. The walls were white and the windows high and arched, glazed with clear, small panes full of little bubbles and ripples. The floor was carpeted in discreet Wedgewood blue, and the cherry pews shone.

The stateliness of the church's design was clearly meant not to fill the worshiper with a sense of the hospitality and grace of a God who delighted in God's people so much as to inspire awe and respect for God's unchanging law. At the same time, paradoxically, there was something about the stark formality of the interior that warned of the dangerous otherness of God which a person would encounter if one were, knowingly or unknowingly, to violate that law.

I was already intimidated by what I saw in my father as the same combination of fixed, often inexplicable law and unpredicatable anger that would blaze out at me when I violated his commands by my deliberate or accidental disobedience. I was also afraid of the equally fixed yet incomprehensible power of my principal and even my teacher at school. It is not surprising, therefore, that the holiness that loomed over me in the sanctuary of my church pressed down on me with its full weight, impressing me with the dangerous qualities of a God who both fascinated and repulsed me.

From the perspective of the eleven-year-old I was, it seemed like an enormous, inhuman building, though I don't believe now that it was. Certainly it was not big enough to contain a room in which my own sixth-grade Sunday school class could meet. That is why the eight or ten children who made up my class assembled at nine-thirty each Sunday morning, not in a separate Sunday school building, far from the risk of contact with a perilous God, but in the front of the sanctuary itself.

It was an intimidating place to meet. I remember that we sat on the right side of the church in a circle of folding chairs on the blue-carpeted, raised platform between the white communion rail and a pedestal on which stood one of a matching pair of gold vases that sometimes held flowers during the worship service. Not far away, beyond the pedestal closest to us, stood the wooden communion table, the offering baskets neatly placed on its shining surface in front and to the side of the empty gold cross that adorned it.

My memory of my Sunday school teacher from that time is hazy. I have a vague impression of a rather plump, middle-aged woman named Mrs. Jones, who didn't know how to make children mind and who couldn't seem to tell us apart. I do remember that she wore patterned silk dresses and round, fussy hats with the kind of wrap-around veils that had little dots woven into them.

What I recall of the other children is much sharper than my memory of my teacher: unfortunately, most of them were boys from my sixth-grade class at school. Having moved from New York to Delaware in the middle of the academic year, and moreover, being excruciatingly shy, I was the perfect target for their cruel teasing. Needless to say, this teasing was not confined to school. If anything, the taunts and pinches were worse and more open in church since Mrs. Jones in her fluffy hats was too oblivious to see them.

My disastrous encounter with holiness occurred on that platform during early spring of that same year. It happened one clear Sunday morning when the daffodils were blooming in the new grass beneath the trees, and the air had the good, cold smell of damp earth. Inside, eight of us, dressed in our Sunday best, sat in a ragged circle behind the communion rail. Mrs. Jones tried to focus our restless energy on the eternal things of God by having us take turns reading out loud the boringly babyish story of Noah's ark. Needless to say, she never told us the worse-than-scandalous following story of Noah and his sons, which would have riveted our attention fast enough!

At any rate, Mrs. Jones's pitiful efforts were in vain. The two or three patent-leather-footed girls rolled their eyes and snickered behind their hands, while the boys, with their slicked-back hair, white shirts, knitted ties, and navy blue suits like their fathers', leaned on the back legs of their metal chairs, stuck their fingers in their collars, whispered loudly, and elbowed one another.

Bored half to death, the two boys on either side of me turned their attention to tormenting me. Furtively, they moved their chairs as close to me as they could get, positioning their Sunday school bulletins so that they could poke me in the sides without Mrs. Jones seeing it. Within a few minutes I was giggling, jerking, and jumping in my chair to escape their fingers.

The end of all this was inevitable. Rocking back to get away from their hands, I tipped over backwards; I was up-ended with the hem of my velvet skirt around my waist and my underpants on display to the hooting boys. Utterly humiliating as all this was, however, this was not the worst of it. As the folding chair on which I sat went down, it crashed behind me into the white pedestal that held the gold vase on our side of the communion table. The pedestal fell away from me, and the vase flew forward. My feet still in the air, I turned my head and saw it lying beside me on the smoky blue carpet. It was cracked neatly in half. I noticed at once, with the peculiar horror you feel when you see the lifeblood gushing out through the skin of an accident victim, that the vase had not been solid, inviolable metal as I had supposed. It had been made, instead, of fragile white china with nothing more than a thin gold glaze over it.

Oh, my friend, I tell you, I have not had many things happen in my life that filled me with as much miserable, raw fear. I no longer recall what Mrs. Jones in her silk dress said, or what my father did when my mother got me home. What I do remember in sharp detail is my terror at the thought of what God would do to me. I knew that my behavior was not only unforgivable, but must certainly draw down the fiercest of punishments. After all, I had violated what was holy, I had committed an act of sacrilege, I had defiled the sacred vessels of the temple, I had desecrated the house of God; for all practical purposes, I had spit on the name of God.

That what I had done had been an accident was irrelevant. I couldn't have been persuaded otherwise. I knew my Bible stories, after all. In the

Old Testament fire had blazed out of the ark of the covenant and killed the people who had only touched it to steady it. If this were true for them, then surely by my own action I had set myself apart for destruction. I went home and waited for months sleepless and sweating for God to strike me dead and send me to hell. Until my parents' divorce the next year when we moved away, just driving by the church on the way to school would make me sick to my stomach.

Of course, the stupidity of grown-ups holding a class of children next to the altar in the sanctuary didn't occur to me. Certainly it never once crossed my mind that God might have looked on me with loving pity for the torment I had already suffered at school and at church at the hands of those boys. Why should it have? The very ongoing nature of my torture and the fact that my parents and my teachers seemed to blame me for it had already convinced me that even God must be offended by who I was.

How I survived the abject fear that followed I can't remember, nor how I came to lose that terrible primitive sense of holiness that I know so often afflicts other children as well. I got no help from the adults in my life; I would never have dared to try to talk to one of them about it.

Somehow, though, I did grow out of much of my childhood fear. As I got older I began to associate the sacred less with the angry power of a dangerous God and more with certain kinds of oppressive human behavior. I can't tell you the content I gave to "hallowed be your name" when I prayed it during that time, or if I continued to pray it at all. I only remember that, to me, holiness was a dreary, perhaps even soul-crushing, business I wanted no part of. To my conservative friends being holy seemed to mean making themselves "pure" by setting themselves apart and above "the world," by not drinking, smoking, playing cards, swearing, or engaging in any form of sex, such as dancing, because, as they said (quoting Paul), "The body is the temple of the Holy Spirit." Did they think that compassion, forgiveness, generosity, or refusal to judge the morals or Christianity of other groups or individuals who disagreed with them had anything to do with holiness? Certainly some of them would have, but I don't recall them saying so.

During the same time, in the more liberal church to which I belonged in high school and part of college, holiness equally appeared to me to be about the preservation of purity. Here, however, purity seemed to be less a matter of setting yourself "apart from the world for God," than of not violating the rules of divinely ratified middle-class social behavior. It never crossed my own mind to associate holiness with compassion, non-judgmentalism, or even justice, though the truly good adults I knew in Highland Methodist Church certainly must have done so. As a girl, rather, I believed that the holy behavior expected of me entailed acting like a lady, wearing a hat and gloves to church, accepting the assigned duties and limits of my gender, not suffering from depression or other embarrassing mental states, not swearing or using vulgarities, and most important of all, avoiding so much as the appearance of sexual impropriety.

"Oh, Roberta," my appalled mother said to me in despair when she was told that I had been seen kissing a boy in the local swimming pool, "what will the neighbors say!" As a sixteen-year-old, I knew I had violated the inviolate just as much as I had when I broke the gold vase in the church in Delaware.

The threatened punishment for such desecration, however, was no longer that I would be struck down by God and sent to hell. The very real threat now was this: if I were perceived to be "loose," no one "nice" would have anything to do with me. I would be talked about and shunned, to become an outcast even in my church. No wonder in those days of the fifties a girl pregnant out of wedlock believed that she "had to" marry the father of her baby, no matter how obvious it was to everyone that she would be miserable with him the rest of her life! What woman would want to subject her family to such disgrace, or put herself in such a position that no decent man would ever marry her?

"Hallowed be your name." My friend, we have the most awful problems in our so-called permissive culture now, but oh how much we suffered and caused others to suffer in the past with such misguided understandings of holiness! It grieves me to recall what a long time it took for me to begin to think of the holiness of God in terms that were not dominated by fear.

Still, did you notice that I spoke just now about *thinking of,* rather than *experiencing,* the holiness of God in other ways? For the fact is, I am convinced that all through my childhood and early adulthood I regularly *was* encountered by God's holiness, though it would never have occurred to me to call it by that name. Rather, in my secret self I named it simply "beauty."

As you already know, I was a difficult child, and from the first grade on I spent as much time as I could reading, daydreaming, not doing my homework or my chores, and resenting my parents and little brother. I mistrusted anyone in authority over me, and I plotted my mild disobediences assiduously. I was always in trouble at home and in school, although I also had a real, though unattainable, desire to "be good" in order to please my parents and teachers.

I disliked the disobedient, resentful child I was. I tried to become good tempered, obedient, hardworking, and docile, but I couldn't do it no matter how hard I tried. My troubles were only intensified by my parents' divorce when I was nearly twelve. I was convinced, as so many children in a similar situation are, that I had driven my father away; and the divorce confirmed my judgment on myself that I was unlovable and morally irredeemable.

It is still amazing that what helped me through those painful years, as well as many grown-up years that followed, were experiences of what the child I was called "beauty." From the time I was the smallest girl, I was rescued repeatedly from my misery and comforted by the secret sight of certain colors. Mostly, these saving colors appeared in some object that let the light shine through: a piece of glass, pale green or dark blue, that I had picked up in the grass outside our apartment; red Jello in a bowl with peaches in its depths shimmering on the kitchen counter; or transparent marbles veined with yellow or turquoise.

But it wasn't only color and light that could have this effect on me. Rock and stone, too, drew me out of myself: a small chunk of red granite I had been given; a mirrored piece of shale I picked up when my parents took us to Manhattan to visit the spot where they were digging the foundations of the United Nations building; a hunk of petrified wood that I could see for myself had once, millions of years ago, been an actual tree growing in a forest.

Later, this saving beauty came to me in music: certain sounds of my flute or the excruciatingly moving melody in a Mozart French horn concerto played on the cheap record player in the room I shared with my mother. As I grew older still, it would often seize me in the narrative of a novel or the shining, searing lines of a poem. When this would happen the strength of these words heard only in my head was so great that, at least for a little while, they were able to empty me both of my sharp pain and my dull depression and fill me instead with an alert and happy awe.

I never thought to associate any of these experiences with the holiness of God. Certainly, I didn't imagine that they had anything to do with what I was praying for when I prayed "hallowed be your name." On the contrary: I was convinced that I wasn't even a Christian because I couldn't believe in the things I had been told in my grandmother's Pond Fork Baptist Church that my salvation depended on.

No matter, however, that I couldn't make this conscious association. An experience of God's holiness is an experience of God's holiness whether we name it that or not, and I am quite sure today that these encounters with saving beauty were, in fact, meetings with the holiness of God. But I'm sure you want to know what makes me say that this is what they were, and not merely some psychological event that originated in my own mind, having nothing to do with God at all.

Besides the fact that they are very like my adult experience of God's holiness, it is because they also had so many of the characteristics of the encounters with holiness I find described in scripture. In the Bible, for example, a meeting with the holy nearly always inspires awe as well as a sense of God's transcendent otherness. Think of Moses at the burning bush, Isaiah in the Temple, the disciples at the Transfiguration, the singers in the book of Psalms. Though I was certainly not a prophet, a disciple, or a psalmist, from the time I was a child this awe was an important part of my response to "beauty." Understand here that I don't mean "awe" to be a synonym for the terror that seized me when I broke the vase in church in the sixth grade. Rather, it was a sense of wonder, quite literally, at the Wonderful that for me carried with it something like a heart-knowledge of the reality of a mysterious, transcendent goodness.

Then there was the quality of grace that always came with these encounters; and grace, according to scripture, tradition, and certainly my own experience, always comes as gift. Even as a child I well knew that this saving beauty was a gift. Encounters with it brought the same feeling I had when I received a present I really wanted: intense happiness and the knowledge that I was loved by the one who had given it to me. I responded to beauty with a gratitude that, given how hard thankfulness was for me as a child, itself felt like a miracle.

These experiences of the beauty of holiness really did come only as gifts; they were never mine to command. I might well find a piece of colored glass in the dirt, wash it in the bathroom, sneak into the bedroom, then hold it up to the window to look through it. What I would experience, however, I knew was never of my doing. Sometimes holy beauty came to me, and sometimes it didn't. Even when it did come, I hadn't always summoned it. Like Sarah and Abraham's unexpected visitors under the oak at Mamre, more often than not, it came when I was least expecting it, in the transparency of the air right before the rain, or in the shape of a tree naked of its leaves.

These experiences had another biblical characteristic as well. In both the psalms and the prophets, encounters with God's holiness bring with them an ability to see ordinary human values, especially of riches and poverty, success and failure, in a new light. Somehow, for me too, when beauty would encounter me, it would nearly always carry with it a sense that, however insignificant, incompetent, and even "bad" I was compared to the strong, competent grown-ups in my life, in the presence of this saving beauty, indeed, even remembering the experience of it later, I was not worthless or "of no account." That I couldn't say to whom my life was valuable, or what its value, hardly mattered.

Holy beauty made its own demands. That an encounter with God's holiness calls forth something corresponding in us is certainly biblical. In the book of Leviticus, God commands the children of Israel to "be holy as I am holy," and it is echoed all through the Old Testament and the New, as well as in many of the commentaries on the Lord's Prayer from the early church.

Even when I was a small child, holy beauty filled me with a longing to be worthy of it, not in order to please others but because I loved it. Now, my friend, notice that I don't say that I felt an *obligation* to be good or a *fear* that I would be punished in some cosmic way if I weren't. What I did believe, however, was that if I were mean to my brothers, resentful of my parents, judgmental or without compassion toward my classmates (all of which I frequently was), I might lose my *capacity* to see it. To put it simply, I loved it and I wanted it, and I was convinced, like the ancient Christian and non-Christian Platonists before me, that "like is only known by like," that if I refused to share its qualities, I could well be left without it.[1]

There was one other striking characteristic of these early encounters with holiness. I never thought to anthropomorphize the God who met me in them. Thinking about this for the purpose of writing to you, it still seems very strange to me that it didn't even occur to me to assign sentience or feeling to this beauty. After all, I all too easily assigned emotions to every leaf-shedding tree, to each pebble kicked around the pavement by a human foot.

What I met filled me with awe and respect, yes; it came to me as a gift; it grounded me in a universe in which I thought I had no place; I loved it and it called forth both a desire and an ability to feel compassion and to love in return; but I didn't connect it with any human personality, certainly not with gray-bearded God or the clean, smiling Jesus I heard about in church.

---

1. Gregory of Nyssa, for example, who wrote after the great persecutions of the early church, explained that what Christians pray for in "hallowed be your name" is an ability to mirror the characteristics of God so that anyone looking at us can see in us something of who God is. (*The Lord's Prayer*, p. 48.)

Since Christians are committed to take the Incarnation seriously, should this mean, therefore, that what I experienced was less than God, God only by analogy? I do not believe it was. Our whole tradition, after all, affirms that the God who came among us in human form paradoxically is also so beyond all human categories of ordinary reason and experience that human language can't stretch far enough to describe God.

Furthermore, Origen in the third century stated that God does come to different people in different ways, according to what we are able to receive. I believe my own childhood anxieties and fear of adults made it impossible for me to receive a God I could only imagine would judge and reject me. I know that there are many people whose experience makes an anthropomorphic image of God impossible for them. All kinds of folk tell me about such difficulties with their prayer—rape victims, but also adults who suffered the childhood loss of a parent by death, divorce, or abandonment; grown-ups whose parents were not able for a whole variety of reasons to give them the attention they needed to be nurtured.

Of course the God who loves us is not going to leave any of us without the very thing we most need, which is Godself. God finds a way through. For me, it was in the experience of beauty; for others, it may be in something very different: in the joy of music, in the love of a pet, in an encounter with nature. I think it is a real issue for Christians that, so often rather than helping folks to recognize such experiences of God and receive them with joy, we tell them that unless they primarily relate to God in terms of Jesus, then they aren't relating to God at all. Why do we insist on doing this? Don't we really believe in God's unswerving, never-abandoning love for human beings? God forbid that I should so deny God's holy appearance in someone else's life!

But all this leads me to tell you about another kind of encounter with God's holiness I have had over the last few years which generally helps me now when I pray "hallowed be your name." Nine or ten summers ago I began to participate regularly in consultations at the Institute for Ecumenical and Cultural Research in Collegeville, Minnesota. From the start, one of the first tasks the twenty or so Institute members were given was to introduce ourselves by telling our individual stories. We were not, however, simply to tell them any way we chose. Rather, we were to take our own understanding of the assigned topic for the year—for example, the content of Christian hope or the meaning of the Incarnation—and use it as a lens through which we would examine our lives and recount them to one another.

In the beginning, this was not easy for me. First, my family upbringing made talking about myself in personal terms hard for me. I grew up in a home where discussing painful private matters, particularly religious ones, was thought to be more tasteless than belching at the table. In fact, it was very nearly considered to be immoral.

This attitude had been reinforced in the sixties by my graduate education in seminary and at Oxford. In both places the importance of putting aside one's individual experience and commitments for the sake of rationality, "real theology," and objectivity was stressed. I had spent years trying to ignore my own experience when I talked about anything of significance to me. Thus, though by this time many life-changing things had happened to me through my prayer, it is hardly surprising that I had never even told myself the story of my life as a religious narrative.

Finally, it had never occurred to me to value the story of my own life; in this context it seemed self-centered even to talk about it. It had been suggested to me enough times over the years that the everyday stuff of ordinary people's lives, particularly if they were the lives of women, was not only without interest, it was faintly ridiculous. Why would any serious person want to hear about my attempts at growing up, wrestling with God, making friends, losing my father, reading, teaching, getting married, having children, doing laundry, getting divorced, falling in love, marrying again, struggling with my wounds, trying to love, being loved, praying, shopping, and cooking?

It was all too hard. Still, even during that first summer at the Ecumenical Institute, the prospect of telling my own story drew me. Other people's stories, from *The Snow Queen* through *The Brothers Karamazov* to *The Fear of Flying*, after all, had formed me from my earliest childhood. As for stories of God, though as I said we didn't talk religion in the home when I was growing up, I had learned in Sunday school and vacation Bible school to understand myself and the world around me in religious terms. Abraham leaving Ur, Jacob wrestling with the angel, Joseph sold into Egypt, Ruth—these stories had always shaped how I saw myself.

That first year, telling my own story was excruciatingly painful. Still, awe and wonder seized me as I listened to the narratives of the other participants' lives. To hear how the long lines of grace, betrayal, pain, faith, doubt, love were interwoven in similar and unique ways throughout the everyday details of each of our lives; to speak of them truthfully, in terms not just of our *convictions* but of our *experience* of God, was deeply wonderful. How could I ever have thought the ordinary facts of any human life were insignificant?

It was only upon my return from Minnesota at the end of the second year's meeting that I could begin to articulate what I was learning from all this storytelling. The day after I flew home, I was in our seminary bookstore, looking over a copy of Athanasius' *On the Incarnation*, which I intended to use for teaching in the fall, when all of a sudden I realized I was wonderfully, unexpectedly happy. I know that no happiness is ever something to take for granted, so I returned the book to the shelf and stood there, puzzling over where this happiness had come from.

Then it came to me. It was from telling and hearing my own story. For the first time I could remember I was truly glad to have lived my own life rather than someone else's. I was not saddened, grieving, or angry for the things I'd lost, done wrong, or been unable to do. I was filled with awe at the continuity of my deepest desires. I marveled at God's grace, which I had never before recognized as grace. I had not seen how the traits and feelings in myself that I had most despised, my childhood anger, my secrecy, my inability to believe what I was told, or my later inability as a woman to live the life set out for me, all had been gifts of God to my deepest self. Though they had often resulted in sin, they were not themselves sin. Like Jacob's wound, they hurt, and they left me limping afterward, but they had also been a source of strength that had both preserved my spirit in demoralizing circumstances and shaped and empowered my adult work.

Standing there by the shelves in the school bookstore, I saw my life held up before me, and I was filled with amazement that came to me on waves of joy. As I had once held up to my eyes the broken pieces of colored glass and been overcome with the beauty that came to me through it, so now I found myself looking through the transparent colors of the story of my chipped and jagged-edged life, and the light of that same mysterious, saving holy beauty was pouring through it.

How could I respond to the holiness of God made visible in me? I was filled with profound gratitude to God and love for the life I had scorned, and I longed to be worthy of this beauty that had been shown to me in it.

But, oh, my friend, all this is so hard to put into words. I do hope that you can see that I am not talking about any holiness here I acquired myself. The holiness I am pointing to can never come from doing or believing the right things, or even from being the right kind of person. Unlike what I thought when I was a teenager, it certainly isn't about being socially acceptable.

Rather, in God's profound love and valuing of my life and every other human life, this holy beauty is simply given. Doesn't the very fact of the Incarnation declare God's love of the ordinary as well as the extraordinary parts of our lives? Jesus himself says it: God not only knows and cares about the fall of the smallest bird in the sky; God knows the very number of hairs on our heads and values them.

Now don't get me wrong. I certainly don't mean by this that I think that everything that ever happens to us, the bad and the good, has been planned by God in advance, and so it is sacred. Though there have been those throughout the Christian tradition who have seen things in this way, I don't believe it for a minute. What I do mean is that my life as a human being, made in the image of God, is holy because God loves it and has always loved it, and so in some mysterious way it is the site of God's beloved, holy presence.

A Place to Pray

In that encounter with the holiness of God, with the *beauty* of the holiness of God, was I given a glimpse of my life as only God can see it "in heaven," in the eternity of God? Do I believe I was granted a hint of the way God holds and keeps the missing memories of my life as my mother holds the memories of my babyhood I can never have myself? This is precisely what I do believe.

My awareness of God made holy in the long lines of the story of my life has never completely faded since that summer eight years ago. It continues to be transforming for me in all sorts of ways, all of them related to how I now pray the words of our prayer, "hallowed be your name."

For one thing, it gives me a means to pray for the healing of my ability to love. It helps me not to turn away from my memories as witnesses against me, but to treat them with respect, as sites, always, of God's holy, mysterious presence. It aids me in gathering in and embracing in myself what I may have wanted to cast off my whole life. "Hallowed be your name," I pray as I struggle with specific hurts and humiliations of my childhood. "Let me see your holy beauty in the child I was when I was twelve."

It also allows me to back off from my own perfectionism, which is an expression of the conviction that I must earn the right to breathe the air. "Hallowed be your name," I pray: "help me know truly that I do not have to prove that I am a person of value. My life is already holy to you, may I make your name holy by accepting my own worth with gratitude."

The goal of the Christian life is not self-love for its own sake, however, but the love of God and neighbor, and praying this prayer in the memory of this beauty helps me do it. Let me give you an example or two. In the fall at the beginning of the school year, I am still sometimes horribly nervous when I stand up for the first time before my one-hundred-and-sixty-student church history class. What if they hate what I say or compare me to better teachers? My fear tends to make me irritable. "Hallowed be your name," I pray in response; "my God, show me a glimmer of your holy, mysterious beauty in each of them so I may lay aside my own anxieties and be with them in the way they need."

But this doesn't happen only at school. I've told you that on my mother's side I was born into a huge family of powerful Kentucky farm women. For most of my life I hated staying on my grandmother's farm and hearing what seemed to me to be the dreary stories of these women's lives. I didn't want to hear about their skills, their intelligence, their faith, and their strength. All of it intimidated and shamed me. What I wanted was to stay away.

My desire to escape them mysteriously began to change, however, shortly after I first was able to see the beauty present in my own life. I was visiting my mother's house in Louisville, and my aunts and remaining great aunt had driven up for the day from Union County to see us both. After lunch ("dinner," they call it on a farm) the women in my family started in on the familiar stories as they cleaned the kitchen. Once more I listened to the stories of doing laundry in an iron kettle in the yard of House on the Hill, of my grandmother's father's manic depression ("being on his high horse"), of my great-grandfather's attempts to steal my uncle Bob from my grandmother, and so forth.

It was before we even got to the pots and pans that I realized I was hearing these ancient accounts in a new way. Rather than feeling judged by them, I was filled with awe and reverence at their beauty and fragility. What would happen to the memories of these women who were my own family? How could these stories containing the precious details of who they had been and what they had done be lost when my aunts and my mother died?

At first, I was overcome with sadness. Then it came to me. I knew these stories; I had learned them against my will. As best I could, I myself would preserve them and the beauty they contained. Soon after, with the help of my mother and my aunts, who encouraged me, I began on a manuscript I call *Houses*. In the years that followed, on nearly every day I worked on it, I prayed for my work, "Hallowed be your name: may I see the beauty of your holiness shining in these lives I write about; may my witness honor it."

Do you know, my friend, from the time I started working on it and praying over it, my relationship with my mother and my aunts began to change. I no longer feel that I have to apologize for myself around them or defend myself against them; now I listen to them, visit when I can, remember, and most important, love them.

Very rarely does a day go by now that I don't pray for the compassion and love that comes with an awareness of God's holy beauty in the lives of the other people with whom I share my world. "Hallowed be your name," I pray as I catch myself pushing away the knowledge of what it is like to be poor and demoralized, unable to find a place to live on minimum wages, to provide good food and medical care for your children. "Hallowed be your name," I pray as I read in the paper of crimes, wars, and atrocities committed here and in places far away. "Hallowed be your name," I pray as I vote for school taxes. "Hallowed be your name," I pray; "may I not turn my face away in callousness, judgment, or cynicism from any human life, from anyone who reflects your image, whether it be an image of your glory or of your humiliation."

Dear friend, how grateful I am for the gift of your own existence in my life, for such a friendship in which we can talk openly about our lives with God and the hard and happy things for which we pray. May God always keep in our hearts the knowledge that these words spoken between us are, after all, as much a part of prayer as anything we do.

Praying without ceasing, "hallowed be your name," I ask for God's grace that we may continue together to learn to see and respond with wonder, gratitude, and love to God's holy beauty not only in our own lives, but in the life of every human being who bears it.

As always, blessings. Write soon.

With love,
Roberta

CHAPTER THREE

My friend,

I am sorry to have to begin this letter by telling you that I need you and your prayers. My friend Melissa has been diagnosed with serious breast cancer. Right now she is in the midst of strong, very painful chemotherapy, and if all goes as it should, she will start stem-cell treatment fairly soon. Oddly, or blessedly, considering where you and I have arrived in our reflections on the Lord's Prayer, for the last few days, waking and sleeping, I have been praying "Your kingdom come, your will be done" with every breath I take.

I can't begin to say how much help reflecting on this prayer is giving me—and how good it is for me right now to be able to talk to you about what is on my mind and heart. I need to remind myself continuously that what God "wills" for Melissa—for me with her, and for every other human being God has created—is life in the Kingdom, restored life that is not governed by pain and death.

This isn't something I've always known. Under the influence of the "it-is-a-terrible-thing-to-fall-into-the-hands-of-an-angry-God" country revival preachers I heard when I was a child, I was terrified of God, God's will, and God's kingdom. Because I was not a good girl, I dreaded the thought of the coming of God's kingdom. After all, I would be spending it in hell.

My fears were at their worst when I was nine or ten. Back then, when my family lived in New York City, every summer my mother and we children would ride the train to Union County, Kentucky, to visit my grandparents' farm for a few weeks. Occasionally, my father would take us on the long trip in the car.

One of my earliest memories from these trips is lying flat on the woolly backseat of our old blue Chevrolet, as hot and itchy driving through Kentucky as a summer case of chicken pox. I couldn't see much in the way of hills and fields, cows and ponds, though I could certainly smell plenty. What was visible between my sandaled feet propped up on the window was an unending string of black telephone poles, with long lines of perched birds, laced together along the two-lane highways. Bored half to death, I would try to count the passing poles, holding my eyes open without blinking until the tears rolled down my face.

The other thing that stuck up far enough to be visible as I lay on my back was a succession of intensely interesting, black, message-bearing barn roofs. "See Rock City Atop Lookout Mountain," the first commanded. This I so longed to obey that I would have flung myself from the moving car to see its wonders. "Chew Mail Pouch Tobacco," ordered the second. The very thought of it filled my vision with the wonderfully gross image of my uncle Bob shooting brown tobacco juice between his teeth onto the yellow dust beside his barn. The third message, however, was of a different sort altogether. "Prepare to Meet Thy God," it glared and bullied, blared and whispered until I found myself helplessly caught up in the sight, sound, smoke, and smells of a terrible Last Judgment.

Though I still hope to see Rock City Atop Lookout Mountain before I die, I've neither chewed tobacco nor have I ever had such an urge. But, oh, my friend, how "prepare to meet thy God" has wounded me over the years! How well it fits with all I heard forty-five years ago in Pond Fork Baptist Church's revivals! "The Kingdom is at hand," I still hear Brother Smith shout. "Are you ready to meet your God, to give an answer before the awful judgment seat of the Lamb?"

Even after I became a Unitarian in my adolescent years I could not escape its threats, for such deep images are not simply erased from our minds and bodies by an act of will. The convictions of our hearts have a life of their own which our chosen convictions rarely have.

This was true even after I had started college and thought I had gotten over it all. In August of 1961 I was nineteen years old and as rationalistic

---

as I could be. I had just finished my second year at Iowa State University. I was on my way from Ames, Iowa, to Southern Methodist University in Dallas to complete my degree in English and later to go on to seminary. It was eleven o'clock at night, and my companion and I were driving across Oklahoma in an old rusted-out Volkswagen. The sky was clouded over to an opaque black; what I could see of the landscape was flat and boring; there was no air and it was hot as hades.

I wasn't thinking about much, nor was I really attending to the myriad sounds of summer insects, cicadas, and crickets, rising and falling, roaring and sawing around me like some kind of diabolical machinery. I sat in a daze, waiting for the miles to pass. Then, all at once, I was brought to attention, adrenaline pumping and stomach tied in knots, as the entire sky flashed bright as early twilight. It stayed that way, too, for what must have been about thirty seconds, though it felt like hours.

My fellow traveler pounded his hands on the steering wheel. "O my God," he cried out as the unnatural light began to fade. "They've finally dropped the bomb on Dallas!"

I myself said not one word in reply: in that single moment when the comet flashed across the sky—for this is what it later proved to be—I was out of the safe harbor of my Unitarian rationalism and back again in the familiar sea of terror of my childhood. "Oh, no, no," my heart pounded out as I buried my head below the dashboard and under my shaking arms. "It's the Second Coming, and I'm not ready!"

I was very glad in seminary to learn that there were other ways to think about God's will and the Kingdom. I was happy to be told that, in spite of the presence of these ideas in the New Testament, there was nothing specifically Christian about them. Rather, in the two or three centuries around the birth of Jesus, there had been a widespread expectation among Jesus' fellow Jews that God was about to inaugurate God's rule after first bringing the world to a cataclysmic end.

We students, however, understood that these beliefs were the result of a misunderstanding of the pure prophetic religion of ancient Israel. The prophets, of course, had threatened that the Day of the Lord was coming when God would judge the people, but they had not meant at the end of time in the way I had learned in Pond Fork. Rather, their preaching was of God's demand (God's will) for justice in the present, as well as of God's punishment for those who failed to meet this demand. "Alas for you who desire the day of the LORD," we learned to quote from Amos (5:18-24).

> Why do you want the day of the LORD?
> It is darkness not light;
>   as if someone fled from a lion,
>   and was met by a bear. . . .
> I hate, I despise your festivals. . . .
> Take away from me the noise of your songs;
>   I will not listen to the melody of your harps.
> But let justice roll down like waters,
>   and righteousness like an everflowing stream.

Jesus only confirmed this prophetic preaching and made it more radical, as we could see for ourselves. "Blessed are you who are poor, for yours is the kingdom of God. Blessed are you who are hungry now, for you will be filled," we read, but also "Woe to you who are rich, for you have received your consolation. Woe to you who are full now, for you will be hungry," and "Whoever loves father or mother more than me is not worthy of me."

In those socially active days of the sixties a lot of us translated all this into a belief that Jesus was calling us to turn against both the ordinary middle-class lives of our parents and the religion we had known in our churches, to replace them instead with a total participation in the politics of the Civil Rights movement. It was out of this radical vision we students recited Jesus' prayer. "Your kingdom come," we prayed; "come with a vengeance and vindicate your people; let the poor, the righteous, and the outcasts inherit the earth and utterly destroy the well-off and those among us who do not picket or work in political campaigns." Knowing ourselves to be among the righteous, we called down God's wrath on sinners without a qualm.

As for when and how we thought the Kingdom was to be accomplished fully, we were certain that Jesus expected it at the end of time. Nevertheless, having learned about "realized eschatology" we also believed that Jesus offered life in the Kingdom to us in the present as though the future were already here. However Jesus actually thought about it, to us, earnest and eager as we were, this could only mean that the coming of the Kingdom must depend upon our own work.

"Your Kingdom come, your will be done!" Oh, my friend, it was wonderful in those days after Pond Fork to think that God was more interested in a just world than in heaven or hell. That God wanted the world to be a good place for the poor, that God would desire racial equality more than niceness, would want hunger eliminated and fair laws passed and implemented—all this fit both with my reading of the Bible and the deepest longings of my heart. It fits to this day, for that matter. Still, there was something painfully wrong about the way we understood both Jesus and the prophets with respect to the Kingdom.

You know, in spite of the language of judgment that so often goes with it, I don't think any of us comprehended that as many prophets besides Amos announced it, not to mention Jesus, Paul, and the book of Revelation, before anything else, the promise of the kingdom of God was meant to be Good News for those who embraced it. Coming upon the Kingdom, says Jesus, is like finding a treasure buried in a field. The Kingdom is expansive and inclusive, like a tiny mustard seed that grows into a bush big enough for birds to nest in it. It is like a mysteriously growing bowl of bread dough. It is the one pearl a pearl dealer might happen upon that is so wonderful he gladly sells everything he owns in order to buy it. It is like a wedding, or a banquet of the king to which everyone is invited.

The Kingdom is an infinitely desirable gift God will give in the future, and is already giving us as a gift in the present. The promise of the Kingdom is God's promise that everything that appears to be irrevocably broken will be made whole, every wounded heart healed, every tear wiped from every eye. Or as Julian of Norwich, the medieval English mystic, said, it is God's promise that ultimately, "all shall be well, and all manner of thing[s] shall be well."

We couldn't feel it. In those days, we were far more interested in God's anger, which of course, we shared. Considering that we believed that we were personally responsible for determining whether the Kingdom came or didn't come, we told ourselves that our own scornful rejection of the unrighteous was appropriate. The Kingdom was God's responsibility, true, but God could act only through us. Without us, justice and racial equality would not roll down like waters, nor righteousness like an everlasting stream.

Of course, we were partly right: God does not customarily rain clothes, food, medical care, and jobs from heaven. Now it seems to me that many of us Christians have lost our ability to understand that we really are responsible to see that our society is just, and that those who are in need are satisfied. At the same time, in those days there was something dreadfully arrogant about our assumption that we ourselves should be the ones to sort out sheep from goats. Just as arrogant was our conviction that without us, God was helpless to achieve God's purposes.

This attitude was also demoralizing and depressing to people like me who believed passionately in social justice but could not share our fellow students' optimism. How could we overlook the complexities of the social problems we were confronted with or the smallness of our power in the face of them? Nor did there seem to be room for righteousness for those were unable to be socially active. ("Why are you sitting here uselessly praying in your prayer group?" I later heard a minister who had also been in seminary in the sixties say to a group of eighty- and ninety-year-old women. "You should be out working for the disadvantaged children in the neighborhood.")

Worst of all, this exclusively justice-oriented God we served was not benevolent. Indeed, he was a God as demanding, scornful, perfectionistic, angry, and—dare I say it?—as full of hatred toward those who failed in their duty as any I had ever encountered at Pond Fork Baptist Church. This God did not inspire us by love, but rather by another version of the same old fear and guilt I had grown up with. In the face of such an image of God and of the effort it took to please that God, of course we could not see that the Kingdom Jesus promised both for the present and for the future was something wonderful, not something dreadful.

Do you know, my friend, it seems to me now that it is simply awful that I and so many other people like me should ever have suffered under the weight of either of these visions of God's ultimate demands and intentions for the world God is said to love! Yet we did suffer under them and many of us do, still. In one of her visions the medieval German mystic Gertrude the Great asks Jesus what he thinks of the fact that some of the nuns in her monastery were frequently afraid to take communion because they worried about what God would do to them if they weren't well enough prepared for it.

Jesus answers her plaintively. "I wish my people would not think me so cruel," he replies. What kind of a monster do we really think God is? How could anybody in her right mind love such a raging, demanding God, or pray that this God's kingdom come and will be done?

Still, it is surprising how often I hear people, and even some of my own good seminary students, speak of the will of God in this negative way. They use "God's will" to explain every awful thing that happens in life. To hear them speak, you would think that it is God who deliberately causes hurricanes, car accidents, childhood deaths, lost jobs, fires, disappointments in love, cancer, and even rape in order to punish us or teach us valuable lessons.

Yes, I did say "rape." Deborah, a friend of mine who works with victims of this particularly dreadful variety of personal assault, once told me of a disturbing conversation she had had with a woman I'll call Sarah. Deborah had been called into the hospital very early one morning in winter shortly after Sarah's escape from a night-long rape and torture. The man who assaulted her had followed her home from the mall, crept up the stairs behind her, then pushed into her apartment after her when she unlocked her door. Throughout the long night in which she had been tied to her bed she had never clearly seen his face, and so she could not even describe him to the police.

When Deborah walked into her room at the hospital Sarah was sitting

A Place to Pray

up in bed, her hair still matted and bloody, her face black, and her body bruised and mangled.

"Hello," said Deborah. She was horrified by Sarah's injuries. She was also trying to turn her full attention to Sarah and forget that the unknown rapist could be anywhere, even in the hall outside Sarah's room.

"I've come to see you," Deborah went on. "Do you think you can tell me what happened to you?"

The injured woman would not look up. She shook her head slowly from side to side. Her arms were covered with scratches and bites, and her hands were wrapped in bandages, but she tried to wring them anyway. She gulped and swallowed a few times while tears dripped from her eyes. "I must have done something really terrible for God to have punished me this way," she answered Deborah at last.

Deborah was so astonished and angry at the idea that anybody in the world might believe that this rape was God's doing that she was speechless. Only after the initial rush of her anger wore off was she able to begin a conversation in which she could suggest that Sarah consider whether, far from God's will being the source of her hurt, it had been God's will working within her that had enabled her to do and say the things that had helped her survive the night.

But, my friend, how alien such a strengthening, enlivening notion of God's will is to so many people who would be too kindhearted to treat their worst enemy in the way they assume God chooses to treat them! Grieving Christians fill our churches. They sit there bewildered, cowering before an imaginary God they believe has hurt them for their own good, to "test" them, to make them do something they didn't want to do, or just to punish them. "Accept it," I have heard good people tell themselves and one another all my life; "it is the will of God. After all, 'the one God loves, God chastises.'"

It isn't hard to speculate on where this need to pin disasters on the will of God comes from in us. Part of it, I suspect, is that we can't bear the idea that anything in our lives could simply be the result of human freedom and the way the universe is put together. We need to believe that the significant events of our lives have meaning and are not simply random, are not just bad luck. If disaster strikes us down, perhaps it is better to have a God whose actions we can't understand and who hurts us but is at least in charge.

We are able to find such a God plausible, I imagine, because of the way our earliest images of God are merged with our earliest images of our parents. In the case of even the best of parents, most of us can remember when our parents were big and we were little, and the times they made us do things we didn't want to do, or prevented us from doing what we longed for, and we didn't understand their reasons for it.

"Why do I have to have a tetanus shot?" the shivering six-year-old cries. "Because you don't want to get sick later," the father answers implacably. "But how can I get sick from one little nail?" she replies. The father doesn't answer as the doctor approaches.

"Why can't I have the car to drive to Macon for the ball game? And why is Dad so angry about it, anyway?" the teenager asks.

"Because you're too young, that's why," the exasperated mother answers, "and if you don't want to understand it yourself, I certainly can't explain it to you."

It is also amazing to me how often we want to describe the inexplicable power of our own inner compulsions as the will of God, compulsions that seduce us to give up what we want or to do what would hurt us or somebody else. In the same way, we find it easy to confuse what God wants with the painful internal pressures we often feel to conform to the expectation of our family, church, or culture.

I know of at least one awful marriage that originated in a couple's compulsive conviction that God intended them to marry in spite of the seriousness of their problems with each other. Was this marriage God's desire for them? It is hard for me to believe when I think about their children's present misery as well as their own.

I also sometimes hear students talk in this compulsive way about their call to ministry, and sometimes it isn't at all clear whether the pressure they feel is only inside them or whether it is almost entirely social. Once not long ago an obviously unhappy middle-aged man joined one of my smaller classes. After a few unsuccessful attempts to encourage him to participate in group discussions, I asked him if he'd like to come and talk to me outside of class. He said he would.

Later that day he knocked on the door to my office, and I invited him in. "What's the matter, Steve?" I asked as he adjusted his sad, heavy frame in my low green chair. "I can tell in class that something is wrong."

Steve shifted around a few times. "I hate being in school," he burst out in his south Mississippi accent. His red hair was standing up around his ears on either side of his balding head like twin burning bushes, and his freckles were glowing on his white skin. "I don't want to be a preacher; I can't stand preachers."

"But Steve," I asked him after the flames died down a little, "why do you stay here? Why don't you just quit seminary and go back to teaching school? I know you used to love teaching children."

"Can't go back," he replied, hanging his head.

"Why not?" I said.

"Because the Lord called me into ministry a long time ago, and I said I'd do it," he answered again. "I have to stick by what I promised. I've got to do the will of God whether I want to or not; that's just the way it is."

Stumped, I sat there a little while and thought about the idea that praying "your will be done" could be translated into the idea that the God of Jesus would make somebody devote his entire life to doing something he hated.

"Tell me about when you think you were called," I said at last.

He hesitated, looking a little sheepish, then he started to talk. "It was like this," he began. "I was in church with my mother one Sunday morning when I was about ten years old. It was the day of the year the minister always tried to get more ministers for the church by preaching on 'dedicating your life to full-time Christian service.' I'd spent the night with a buddy the day before and we'd stayed up late eating junk food and watching television, so I was tired and kind of sick to my stomach. The sermon went on and on, and by the time it was over I was practically lying in my mother's lap." Steven stopped and cleared his throat, then he went on.

"After the preacher finished preaching, he had an altar call; anybody touched that day by his message was supposed to go up and dedicate his life to full-time Christian ministry. To help us do this, he told us, we would sing the hymn, 'Trust and obey, for there's no other way to be happy in Jesus, but to trust and obey.' We would keep on singing it, too, until someone came forward and answered God's call.

"Well," he went on, "we sang all the verses, then we sang them all over again, and after that he held up his hand and had us stop.

"He came halfway down the aisle, glared at us for a while, then spoke again. 'I feel it,' he said, dramatically laying his hand on his heart. 'God is calling somebody right now, but that person is resisting. Don't think you can get away with it,' he went on, swiveling his eyes from one side of the room to another. 'Nobody can resist the will of God!'

"The preacher found me in the third row and stared me in the eye. I couldn't turn my head away.

"We sang again, twice, before he stopped us once more. 'All right,' he said, crossing his arms over his chest. He looked at me and frowned with energy. 'You know who you are. I'm going to the back and I'm locking the doors, and nobody is leaving this place till you come on forward.'

"By this time," poor Steve said, "I was clenching my teeth in the pew, waiting to hear what that sucker would say next. Well, I let us sing it three more times, then I gave up. I was hungry and desperate, and everybody wanted to go home. He was bigger than I was, and I figured he'd outlast me no matter what I did, so I went on up and signed away my life." Here Steve stopped and shook his big head wistfully.

"The next thing I knew, everybody in that church from the old ladies to the little children had come up after me; they were grabbing my hands, crying and kissing and congratulating me to beat the band.

"I never, ever, wanted to be a preacher, but from that time on they always called me their preacher-boy and told me how proud they were and how great a preacher I'd make. My mother was proud; the old ladies made me cakes and the old men told me how fine I was. What else could I do? God trapped me plain and simple. It was God's will, and the only

A Place to Pray

mistake I ever made about that was thinking for a little while I could [get] out of it and be a teacher."

It was quiet in the room for a few minutes while I thought about the idea of God tricking somebody into spending his life doing something he hated.

"You know, I don't agree with you about your notion of how God's will works," I said at last, and I told him what I thought of his preacher's manipulation and how the God I knew might regard a promise extorted so shamelessly from a little boy.

Steve still didn't see it as I did when he walked out of my office that day, but he was considering it. By the end of the school year he decided to drop out of school. He's gone back to teaching in Mississippi, and as far as I know, he is perfectly happy.

I cannot believe God is cruel, nor do I think that fear is an appropriate response to God's will. What does fear have to do with our anticipation of God's kingdom? Nothing, except for the fear of missing it altogether because we refuse to participate in it, or of not paying attention to it when it is right under our noses. "Don't be afraid," Jesus again and again tells his followers in the Gospels. "Do not be afraid."

God's kingdom, which comes according to God's will, is a gift, not a nightmare of coercion. God desires our life and not our death. "Do you not realize," Jesus asks us, "that God's kingdom is where God's will is done, and that God's will for you is for your well-being, and for the well-being of all God has created? This is the Kingdom you pray for. If you live in this awareness, then as far as it is possible in this world, you can live now in the Kingdom."

With my tendencies to despair over social problems, coupled with my childhood conviction that I deserved unhappiness, I have always needed this reminder that praying for the kingdom of God, and for the will of God governing it, is an act of hope. There have been so many mornings over the last few years when praying for the Kingdom, in the expectation that the time will truly come when all things shall be healed, was the only thing that got me out of bed. This gets me back to Melissa, her cancer, and how hard it sometimes is these days for me to live in the Kingdom.

Early one chilly Tuesday morning two months ago, the phone rang as I was slaving away on the exercise bike. I picked it up, sweating and puffing.

It was Melissa, who never used to call me before four o'clock in the afternoon, unless it was an emergency, because we were both writing or teaching.

"Hello," Melissa said. Her voice sounded tired and strained. My imagination leaped to attention. Melissa has always been beautiful, long-legged, graceful, and strong, with incredibly blue eyes and smooth brown hair. Now I saw her standing by her desk in her big study, the phone at her ear, her shoulders hunched, and one arm wrapped around her middle.

"What's going on?" I asked.

"Tell me what's going on with you first," she answered. Impatiently, I gave her a quick rundown. Then she couldn't put it off any longer. "Roberta," she said, apologetically. "I'm really sorry to tell you that I have cancer."

I interrupted. "Melissa, are you sure?" I asked, stupidly.

"Yes, I am," she replied. "I went in to the doctor on Friday to have a couple of lumps checked out in my breast. They did a biopsy Friday afternoon. I do have cancer and it's really serious."

Past that point, there was not much she was emotionally able to tell me. Somehow, I got through the rest of the conversation and went on to my teaching. The next few days were terrible. For Melissa they were frantically busy, devoted as they were to tests, innumerable trips to doctors, a visit to the hospital to put in the shunt for chemotherapy, telling her grown children, making arrangements for help from a student, redoing her will, taking a trip out of town to visit her parents, and finally, beginning the chemotherapy. I could hardly get to her.

As for me, I felt like a child who had fallen asleep on a long family car trip only to be awakened from a deep slumber by a hand on my shoulder shaking me. "Wake up now, Roberta, we're here!" Like the waking child, during that first week I was in such a state of bewildered shock that I wasn't sure where I was or whether it was night or day, and the shock was made worse by Melissa's lack of time to talk or visit. Imagining what already was and what was to come, I could hardly think or bring myself to move my body.

Melissa and I have been friends, sisters, really, for nearly twenty years, and we are exactly the same age. In the way only old friends can, we have gone through most of the significant stages of our adult lives together. We have shared our clothes, our pleasures, our secrets, and our crises over our work, our writing, our sons and daughters, our husbands, and our parents. Having learned loss early in life, I had always imagined my own death, as well as the deaths of my parents, my husband, and even my children. But Melissa? After everything else was gone the two of us were looking forward to being old ladies together. For some unfathomable reason, I had never imagined losing her.

As those first days passed and Melissa's time continued to be taken up with preparations for her treatment, my shock began to be replaced by a growing dread of the pain I knew she had ahead of her. At the same time, though I was deeply ashamed of feeling sorry for my own pain in the face of what she was preparing for, I was grieving for myself.

Finally, the day came when we could spend real time together. It was soon after her first chemotherapy treatment. Her hair was already almost all gone, but even under my fanatical scrutiny, she looked like herself. I was so relieved to see her I was euphoric, and she took a real delight in being able to enjoy our day. We spent the morning shopping for pretty dresses, for the things she would wear in the weeks to come, and for several pairs of soft pajamas.

After that, we treated ourselves to lunch in a nice restaurant where she told me what she hoped for herself and what she wanted from me, both in the present and as she saw treatment progressing. As she ate her roast lamb, mashed potatoes, and green beans (my normally abstemious friend was ravenously hungry), she stated that she didn't know what was coming, how many good days she would have, or whether she would die or recover.

was certain, however, that her old life as she had taken it for granted was gone. The old had passed away. Now she was in a New Time, a whole New Age, and she intended to live in it fully and consciously, whatever came next.

She did not wonder, as Sarah had done, why this was happening to her. She did not believe she was being punished, justly or unjustly. "The question," she said to me as she stirred three spoons of sugar into her iced tea, "is not 'why me?' but rather, as a mortal human being, 'why not me?'" She wanted to be as much as she could with the many people she loves. She did not want to waste her time brooding over what might have been, or worrying about things that were of no ultimate concern.

It made me happy to hear her talk—though I must admit that just being with her that day would have made me happy no matter what she said. I was filled with a kind of holy awe and gratitude that she would let me share in what already was and what was coming, whatever the hard times ahead.

Later that night, as I mulled over the morning and afternoon, I understood that with Melissa's decision deliberately to live in this new world, Melissa had chosen the kingdom of heaven which Jesus had announced. Simultaneously, I knew that this was the first occasion in my own life in which I consciously understood the poignancy in the paradox of the promise of this kingdom.

That day, as Melissa spoke of her reaction to the chemotherapy, I had had a glimpse of the inevitable pain that was coming; I knew intimately that her possible death from the treatment or from the cancer was real and wrenching. At the very same time, from the moment I had laid eyes on her that morning, in a new and wonderful way I was also certain of the reality of God's promise that in the Kingdom all will ultimately be healed, every tear wiped away, and everything made new. In the context of dreadful suffering in this mortal life, I knew that being able to set aside worries over the unimportant to give and make ourselves fully receptive to joy, life, and love is to live now in the Kingdom Jesus tells us is at hand. How I wanted this Kingdom, and how I would pray for it for Melissa!

But oh, my friend, how hard some of these days are! Right now, at the

---

end of her fourth round of chemotherapy, Melissa is, indeed, living in the way she had hoped, but she is also more exhausted and wounded than I believe she had imagined. She is grieving for everything and everybody she may be losing. As for me, the promise that "all shall be well and all manner of things shall be well" does not begin to explain away or lessen the reality of Melissa's suffering and grief or of my own.

I find myself suddenly bursting into tears in the most embarrassing of places. Kingdom or no Kingdom, how can I even begin to think of waking up in the morning to know that she is gone? My only consolation is that the God who loves us as friends shared and still shares firsthand in suffering like Melissa's and my own. Even the full knowledge of the coming Kingdom did not exempt Jesus from pain over Lazarus's death, or from having to anticipate his own impending execution with fear and sorrow.

In the face of all this, my friend, believe me when I tell you that I am praying for comfort, strength, and hope, "your Kingdom come, your will be done on earth as it is in heaven." "Loving God," I ask daily, "help me remember what I have learned of you from the work of my prayer, from my teachers of the early church, from scripture, from loving and being loved by Richard, my husband, my children, my friends, my mother, and my father. Do not let me forget that, though 'the last enemy is death,' 'love is stronger than death,' that 'many waters cannot quench love, neither can floods drown it.' Help me remember that I do not need to know the time or the form the ultimate healing of all things will take, but I do know that you, our God, are consistent. You who create, heal, love, and give life right now are the same God who governs the future. You, the God who has not yet abandoned us and whose will for us is life, will not abandon Melissa, or me, in what is to come."

My friend, these days there is not much more to my prayer than this. You can hear that I need you to pray in the hope of the Kingdom for Melissa and for me, too. Remembering you who are also beloved to me, I will pray for you, too.

Roberta

CHAPTER FOUR

My dear friend,

I'm very glad to hear that the problem in your church around the matter of praying the Lord's Prayer is beginning to resolve itself. It is so important that we really understand that prayer is never meant to be an obligation, something laid upon us as a burden we must assume whether we like it or not. Prayer, I believe, insofar as it is conversation with God which is part of the sharing of a common life with God, is far less a duty than it is a gift God gives to us. As the great fourth-century teacher of prayer from the Egyptian desert, Evagrius Ponticus, says, "If you wish to pray, then it is God whom you need. [God] it is who gives prayer to the [one] who prays."[1]

If it is true that prayer in general is given to us by God as a gift of love rather than as an absolute command to conform to what we are told to do, then this must be particularly true of the Lord's Prayer. Jesus, as I understand him in the Gospels, does not do much commanding of the people around him at all. What he does do is call them to a radical new life in the kingdom of God in which they will be able to thrive as God intends. I believe this is the context in which the disciples asked Jesus to teach them to pray, and in response, he gave them this prayer.

And this—the idea of God or Jesus giving us gifts—brings me to the part of the Lord's Prayer you and I are ruminating over at the moment, the first real petition in the prayer, the first actual asking of God for something in it: "give us this day our daily bread." "Give us this day our daily bread"—so easy to say, and, as you point out, so difficult, at one time or another, at least, for most of us to mean!

---

1. Evagrius Ponticus, "Chapters on Prayer," 58, p. 64.

Where shall we start with this petition? If our primary interest were that of scholars of the New Testament who were trying to figure out the exact meaning of "give us this day our daily bread" in its original first-century context, then, of course, I would say that we should begin with the most obscure word, philologically speaking: it is the Greek adjective *epiousios*, the word in the prayer which is ordinarily translated in English as "daily." Certainly, *epiousios* being a word so rare in Greek that neither the writers of the early church nor modern scholars are agreed on its meaning, it is worthy of a lot of attention.

When you ask me in the context of our present ruminations over how we can pray this petition, "give us this day our daily bread," however, I know that your first interest is not the investigation of a technical problem with a single word in New Testament Greek. For that, you would do what you are already doing: going to good commentaries on the Gospels of Matthew and Luke and working on it yourself. Your present concern, rather, is to think about how through praying the words of this petition over a long period of time we can seek healing for the things that get in the way of our growth in the love of neighbor, self, and God.

Because questions having to do with our own prayer are our real interests right now, I suggest we begin with the word "give," the primary word in "give us this day our daily bread" that you tell me causes you problems. As you say in your last letter, it is hard for you to ask anybody, and not just God, for anything. You don't mean asking someone else to wish you luck or pray for you, either. You are talking about asking for something like a ride to the store when the car breaks down, or even borrowing two eggs from a neighbor—something that might "put somebody out."

In your letter you also mention that you are beginning to suspect that this reluctance to ask other human beings for help may be connected with your difficulties in asking God for things in prayer, including even "your daily bread," if you let yourself think about it. You want me to tell you whether I think you might be right about this, and what my own experience has been.

First, let me say that I agree with you completely when you suggest that how we pray—indeed, how we generally relate to God—is always intimately and inextricably connected with how we relate to other people. It is my experience that as much as we would like to have our "spiritual life" separate from and uncontaminated by our "everyday life" among the folks with whom we live and work, the fact is, it is simply not possible. Plenty of us try it, of course; maybe we all need to confess that we are sometimes tempted to pretend that the character of our human relationships has no bearing on how we are with God.

The fact is, however, as long as we genuinely want to be in relation to God as a person (and the very reality of the Incarnation suggests that we do), the same habits of mind and heart that govern the way we are with other human beings are also going to shape the way we are with God, and vice versa. To give an example or two of what I mean: if we are generous, forgiving, and trustful with other human beings, then we almost certainly will also be so with God. If, on the other hand, we are continually critical of the people around us and expect to be criticized by them, we will just as likely primarily relate to God as one to whom we must continually confess our sins and faults. In the opposite direction, if we experience God as unworthy of our trust, the chances are we will find it very hard to trust other human beings as well. Of course, this is bound to have a profound effect on our prayers.

Why should this be true? One obvious reason is that both our unexamined, gut-level images of God and our basic patterns of relating to other people are formed very early in us out of our childhood experiences of parents, grandparents, teachers, or ministers who are in a position of nurture and authority over us. Even in the fourth century, Gregory of Nyssa talked explicitly about the way in which these childhood experiences shape our adult relationship to God. Take the case of two abandoned little girls raised in two different households, one by a Christian lady careful to teach her of the love of God, the other in a brothel where she was a child prostitute. How could the difference in their rearing not be reflected in their relationship to God, and how, says Gregory additionally, could

God possibly fail to respond to the second with extra compassion and understanding?

I think another reason for the similarity between our relationship to God and that of our relationship to other people has to do with what it means to be made in the image of God. Have you ever considered the idea that all our relationships—to our mothers, our friends, our spouses, our fathers, our siblings—are, in fact, only images, in many cases damaged images, of our primary relationship with God, who is much more fundamentally our mother, friend, spouse, father, not to mention our sister and brother? For me this is the implication of Ephesians 3:14, 15, which speaks of God as the father from whom every family takes its name.

But to get to the next part of your question: you want to know if I myself ever had the kind of trouble asking people for things you speak of in your letter. Believe me, my good and honest friend, I most certainly have, and all my life, too. I remember in excruciating detail the day twenty-three years ago when I first became aware that I had a problem here.

I was in the process of remodeling an old house in the city where I used to teach when I became pregnant with my son Benjamin. Me being the vomiting sort of expectant mother, if you recall, the first few months of my pregnancy were horrible. The house needed to be finished by a particular date so that we could move into it, but for various reasons, I was the only one prepared to work on it.

I managed by working even harder than I could, frequently climbing down off the scraping, hammering, and painting ladder to throw up. More significantly, I also hired various graduate students to come in over the summer to assist me with the hardest jobs. This worked well at first; the students really helped, and I was very glad to pay them a better than average wage for what they did. Soon, however, school started, and they all had to quit—all, that is, but one.

The remaining one was a typically poor Old Testament graduate student named David Clark. David would simply show up at my rundown door two or three times a week. Each time we would have the same conversation.

"Roberta," he would announce, his hands in his pockets, "I have three hours to work. What do you need me to do that you can't do yourself?"

I would always reply the same way. "David, I have so many things you could do I can hardly list them. I'm so grateful for your help; I can't imagine how I would have done it without you so far. I know you don't have any money. You simply must let me pay you."

David, irritated, would never let me pay him, and anxiously I would finally give up and let him scrape a ceiling, nail up Sheetrock, or paint the laundry room. As the weeks passed and he kept on coming, however, the two of us grew more and more frustrated with each other.

One day while David and I were having our usual conversation, David had as much of my attempt to pay him as he could take. He crossed his arms over his paint-covered plaid flannel shirt and looked up at me as I stood on the seat of a backless green kitchen chair, my big belly poking out in front of me as I chipped away at the old brown plaster on a bedroom wall.

"Okay," David said. "It's time to come down off that chair. You and I are going to have a talk."

Nervously, I climbed off the chair; then he took me rather roughly by the shoulder and sat me down.

"You make me so angry when you keep offering to pay me," he began. "Have you ever stopped to think what it says about you that you don't want anybody to do anything for you unless you pay them for it? You do things for other people all the time. If you don't let them do things for you, it is hard to avoid concluding either that you think you ought to have the moral upper hand by not owing anybody anything, or else that you are afraid they might ask something of you in return."

"No, no." Already convicted, I tried to interrupt him, but he ran right over me.

"I'll bet you tell yourself it's Christian not to ask for anything or let anybody give you help, don't you?" he said; it wasn't really a question.

"No, no," I answered again, weakly. I was lying, and he knew it. At some level I did think it was Christian for me not to ask for anything, or at least, not to want or need anything.

David kept on. "Where does it say anything like that in the Gospels? Just show it to me! Your whole life depends on other people as well as on God. Everything worth having comes to you as a gift! Haven't you ever heard of grace?"

My friend, by the end of this conversation I was absolutely stricken. I had begun to learn some things about myself I hadn't realized before. I was mortified to realize that a significant part of me did intend to pay the students because I hadn't wanted to "be beholden" to them, and I really didn't want to feel that their generosity might give them a moral advantage over me. Just as bad—and I was glad David didn't know this—I didn't really like them to do things for me because it humiliated me to admit my need. And I had hidden all this, as well as my own lack of generosity, from myself by telling myself how Christian I was being. In fact, I had patted myself on the back for righteously trying to live out the saying that "it is more blessed to give than to receive."

Believe me, my friend, I took David's words to heart that day. I mulled over them, I began to meditate on the difference between the great American virtue of self-sufficiency and independence, and the Christian virtue of acknowledging our dependence and receiving everything that comes to us with a grateful heart. I asked myself why I found it humiliating to be in need, when I knew perfectly well that all of us are continually in need of one another because that is the way God made us. Then I began to repent.

Not that I overnight became a person who could ask and gracefully receive from others: the Abbas and Ammas of the Egyptian desert are right, of course, when they warn us that such damaging wounds to the spirit heal very slowly, and even then, only when, with the grace of God and of other people in our lives, we work hard at our own healing.

In fact, I was making progress with the moral-upper-hand part of my problem, but I also was still wrestling with the other parts of this problem when I married Richard many years later. I was still suffering from the miserably misguided idea that, while other people in my life wanted and needed things from me, if I were a Christian and a good person, I really ought not to want or need anything from them. It really used to strain our love that I could never bring myself to ask Richard directly to do something for me or tell him what I wanted.

Interminable, explicit, and needless to say, painful discussions with Richard on this subject helped a lot. So did my prayer, once I had established something like a regular discipline, because it was there in that space that I began to be able to think about where my gut-level ideas concerning asking and receiving had come from. In the sustaining presence of God I could let myself remember how hard asking for something from my parents nearly always was when I was an elementary school student. Part of it, I know now, was because they didn't have much money, and it angered them that they often couldn't give me or do for me what I wanted. On top of that, however, it always pierced my conscience when I heard them telling each other how my generation was certainly going to the dogs because we "had too much." As an added factor in the development of my difficulties around asking for things was my step-grandmother who used to give me piles of nice presents for Christmas, but then would so mercilessly criticize the writing of my thank-you letters that I still almost can't write letters. In my prayer I remembered, too, the context in which my mother had told me "never to be beholden to anybody for anything." It was in the fifties after my parents were divorced when Mama's wounded pride made her particularly and understandably resistant to being patronized.

Now, my friend, don't get me wrong. I am not telling you about my childhood in order to blame the adults in my life for my later difficulties. I am quite certain that I was loved by parents and even a step-grandmother who were seriously concerned for my welfare. My need to find the causes of my difficulties here, as is true for everybody, was to understand the past not for its own sake, but in order to grow in love of God, neighbor, and self in the present and in the future. Abba Poemen used to say, "It is not understanding what has happened that prevents us from going on to something better,"[2] and I believe it, deeply. Bringing "what

2. Poemen 200, *Sayings of the Fathers,* p. 194.

has happened" into my conscious mind gave me a way to evaluate and start revising what I believed, and equally important, to begin to practice other ways of being.

Oddly enough, considering the deprivation they all chose to live under, meditating in my prayer on how the words of some of the desert Fathers and Mothers contradicted my own training also helped me significantly to learn to receive. One saying that I spent a great deal of time with was the paradoxical one of Abba James: "It is more blessed to receive hospitality than to give it."[3] Another, longer one was this:

Some old men were entertaining themselves at Scetis by having a meal together; amongst them was Abba John. A venerable priest got up to offer drink, but nobody accepted any from him, except John the Dwarf. They were surprised and said to him, "How is it that you, the youngest, dared to let yourself be served by the priest?" Then he said to them, "When I get up to offer drink, I am glad when everyone accepts it....That is the reason, then, that I accepted it, so that he also might...not be grieved by seeing that no-one would accept anything from him." When they heard this, they were all filled with wonder and edification at his discretion.[4]

Both of these sayings, illustrating the importance to the giver of having her gift received, jolted my attention away from my own "oughts and ought nots." How many times had I been offered something to eat or drink at somebody's house, and I had disappointed the one doing the offering with, "Oh no, don't make trouble for yourself"? How many times had Richard given me a gift or done something for me and I had half ruined it by insisting, "You really shouldn't have"? How had I robbed David all those years ago when I could not receive with graciousness what he offered me?

I also got some real help from the Gospels. I thought of how happy Jesus seemed to be to ask and receive from others without appearing to

---

3. James 1, *Sayings of the Fathers,* p. 104.
4. John the Dwarf 7, *Sayings of the Fathers,* p. 86.

worry either about seeming weak or about "being beholden." I tried to imagine being one of those women Luke mentions who went around with him and paid the bills for his ministry. I also mulled over both Jesus' insistence that the disciples let him wash their feet and his warning to Peter, who was refusing him, "Unless I wash you, you have no share with me."[5]

At the same time, I pondered Jesus' explicit teaching about asking God for things, like the parable of the man at midnight who makes his friend get up and disturb the whole household in order to give him a loaf of bread and the parable of the widow who keeps asking the unjust judge for justice until she finally wears him down.

Last, I turned over and over in my mind the way Jesus' flesh-and-blood friends Mary and Martha weren't satisfied simply to ask Jesus to help them when Lazarus got sick, but pushed him; how even after their brother's death, they refused to take no for an answer, and how Jesus responded in the end, not by rebuking them, but by raising Lazarus from the dead.[6]

All of this helped me greatly when it came to asking and receiving from the other people in my life, but there was more even than this to my problem with petitionary prayer to God, and this brings me to my own questions I still wrestle with, questions that have to do with the way in which we are to understand petitionary prayer itself.

How are we to think of petitionary prayer? When I was a little child, I never worried about why or how I prayed before I went to sleep. I prayed because it was what good children did, and I asked God for the things I knew the adults around me wanted me to ask for. "Please feed the hungry children in China," I would pray; "if I should die before I wake, I pray the Lord my soul to take"; "God bless Daddy and Mama and Freddie and Wesley, and everybody else in the world"; "give us this day our daily bread."

---

5. John 13:8.
6. John 11.

It wasn't only things I asked for, either. God was a God of raw power and might, and I also prayed in order that such a potentially dangerous God would keep my family, me, and my familiar world safe for another twenty-four hours. My childhood prayer was an entreaty, but it was also a magic ritual for manipulating God, in the same category with not stepping on a crack in the sidewalk because everybody knew, "step on a crack, break your mother's back." Did I pray in those so-called innocent days for a bicycle or a stuffed animal I selfishly wanted just for myself? I probably did, but I'm sure I felt as guilty about it as I would have if I had directly asked for these things from my parents.

When I got a little older and more sophisticated, I knew I had to learn to pray in a more adult way, but learning was harder than you might think. In church I heard people talk about petitionary prayer in three other ways, and none of these seemed satisfactory or even, for that matter, plausible.

The first way seemed to me to be another variety of my childhood magical approach to prayer. From what I heard, it would appear that you could manipulate God into giving you what you asked by making yourself really, really believe that God would give it to you. This was called "having faith," and how much faith you had was measured by how much of what you prayed for you got. Do you remember all that mustard-seed jewelry we used to wear in the fifties?

"If I had only had enough faith when I prayed," I once heard an utterly defeated woman say, "Mother never would have died." I hated it! If mother dies and it's my fault, it gets God off the hook, of course, but what kind of a diabolical God is it who would make my mother's life dependent on me being able to perform some trick on myself to make me believe what seems to me to be impossible? What God would blame me for not being able to lie to myself successfully?

Probably the same cruel kind of God I heard another person talking about when he said, "After Daddy had his stroke, I prayed that God would spare his life. Well, Daddy lived, all right, but now he is going to spend the rest of his life in a coma. You'd better be careful what you pray for, you know. God might just give it to you!" None of this was for me.

From other people in church I also heard another way to think about asking God for things. This was petitionary prayer as the expression of a contract a person makes with a God who exercises absolute control over everything that happens in life. "Yes," I used to hear our lay leader preach on layman's Sunday, "I told God, if God would only see to it that I got this job, I would tithe 10 percent of my income the rest of my life." Sadly, I would hear just as frequently, but never in church, "I don't believe in God anymore; I told God I would quit my job and go into ministry. God still let my daughter die."

Even as a teenager I could see the advantage to this approach: it gives the sufferer someone, namely God, to blame when inexplicable things happen. At the same time, it makes some odd and unbiblical assumptions about what God is like and how we are to relate to God. It assumes, for example, on the one hand, that my commitment to God is a kind of cosmic insurance policy to which I am entitled to pay extra premiums in times of crisis to guarantee that God will make things turn out the way I want them. On the other, it assumes that God is the sort of God who actually would save a child's life only because her father paid God for it. How could I accept that?

Not surprisingly, I never heard these unsatisfactory approaches to petitionary prayer recommended by a minister from the pulpit. What I did hear from the time I was a child was an approach that was, in fact, quite in keeping with large portions of the Christian tradition but, for very different reasons, was equally unsatisfactory for me. One of these reasons had to do with how the picture of the God to whom I was to address my petitions intersected with my deepest personal experience. This God I heard about was, practically speaking, male (not that I was told this overtly), an All Powerful and Perfect Ruler of the Universe who had a personal interest in me and yet had no need of me or anybody else, who hated my sin, and who knew my every thought. This was a God whose ways were not my ways nor thoughts my thoughts. The conclusion the various preachers reached about God's incomprehensibility was not, however, as it suggests in Isaiah, that God is so much more compassionate than human beings, but that we human beings are never in a position to question such a mighty, blindingly powerful, and righteous one. To him who was both my creator and my judge, what I owed was not questioning but trust and obedience.

None of this was really implausible to me—far from it. Rather, God was very much like my own strict father, only even bigger, more demanding of obedience, more discerning, more offended by what I did wrong, more fascinating. God was certainly even more likely to respond to my requests with anger than my father. (Do you remember what I said earlier about the way I believe we form our childhood images of God in the image of those who nurture and have authority over us?) It wasn't that I couldn't believe in or seek intimacy with such a God because this God was unbelievable. It was, rather, that I was afraid of this God who might destroy me if I got too close.

Back in the sixties when I was in seminary, all my anxiety about prayer was put to rest, at least for a few years, when I decided that it wasn't even appropriate to ask God for anything because there couldn't be any grounds in the modern world for believing in a personal God who intervened in the world, anyway. I wasn't alone in my conclusions, either. Those were the days, as I've told you before, when most of my classmates believed that, if we were to take the laws of nature, science, and human rationality seriously, then we were also bound to accept the illogicality of expecting that God would break those intricate laws of cause and effect for the sake of the desires or needs of a single individual or group. To ask God to intervene anywhere was precisely to ask God to break the laws of nature. Petitionary prayer, therefore, could never be more than an exercise in narcissism and intellectual dishonesty. Why would we think God would heal one woman of cancer and let the woman in the bed next to her die? God didn't play favorites, and God wasn't particularly interested in sickness, anyway. Insofar as God could be said to have a concern, it was, as the Old Testament prophets said, for justice and righteousness in the whole of society. Petitionary prayer was fine, therefore, but only if it was for something like world peace or racial equality.

For a long time, really through the first years of my present teaching job, this is what I believed both because I thought I had no other honest intellectual option, and because it gave me so much relief from my earlier, distantly rejecting and judgmental images of God. Then, gradually, I began to find that, whatever natural law might govern the world I lived in, what I considered to be the only possible way to understand prayer wasn't working for me.

For one thing, I was under a lot of internal pressure with respect to my job and my family. For another, in the early monastic literature I taught, I had heard and continued to hear about a very different God who was, in fact, neither an impersonal, unemotional God confined by the fixed laws of nature or a distant, judgmental father who asks for absolute obedience. The God my ancient teachers showed to me was, rather, one who at the same time was infinitely mysterious and an intimate lover of individuals. This was a God who draws (and was drawing me) into relationship, a God who was tolerant of human weakness of all sorts in a way no human being in my life ever had been.

This new knowledge and experience gave me an alternative life-giving image of God with which I might begin to replace the one that I had struggled with in childhood, one that had come out of the very tradition itself if I could only accept the idea of a God to whom I could personally relate. But how could I come to accept the possibility of a personal God and still hold on to my modern view of the world?

What the great teachers of ancient Christianity told me was that nobody gets to know God by first intellectually working out the answers to his or her problems and then by praying, but that one gets to know God by praying first, taking risks in prayer as we gradually come to share a common life with God. Would I make a friend of a person I'd never met but only heard about by reputation, by concluding what sort of person she would have to be, and then, still not having met her, making up my mind whether I would be friends with her? Of course not! I would meet the actual person, get to know her face to face, then see what developed.

At this point in my life, I was desperate and so I jumped, full of the most serious doubts even about my own honesty, into a discipline of daily prayer that included the elements of the kind of prayer I had learned about from my teachers in the ancient Christian desert. There were a lot of psalms, a little gospel, conversation with God (how hard that was to learn, considering how terrified I was of God when I began), often agonizing introspection and wrestling with my fears and angers in the light of my own history and the ancient monastic sayings, and finally, a lot of silence.

In the context of that prayer over a long period of time, I began to be able to exchange many of my doubts as well as my older, hurtful personal image of God for a firsthand experience of the generous and intimately gentle God I know today—and, just as you would have predicted, my friend, at the same time I also began to give up my own fearful judgmentalism toward myself and the other people in my life, including my father. What a gift to each other we both were in his last years, and how very much I miss him!

"But what about the rest of it?" I can hear you asking. "Didn't you still live in the same modern world governed by fixed scientific law that had made you reject a personal understanding of God in seminary? You might have experienced God as personal, but weren't you still convinced that God was unable to bend the laws of cause and effect in your behalf or anybody else's no matter how you prayed? Didn't you think your prayer, in other words, was just as self-deludingly narcissistic as ever?"

The fact is, I did still live in the same universe, but I came to recognize the inconsistency in my own thinking with regard to how fixed it actually is. Since undergraduate school I had taken it for granted that the whole physical universe is put together like a piece of machinery, so that if a person or God were able to know all the most minute natural laws governing it, everything that happens or ever will happen would be perfectly predictable. Now I could recognize that I'd never been thoroughgoing in this. I had been sure about the obviously material realm: diseases and their cures, for example, operated according to the inexorable laws of cause and effect, but with respect to the human heart, that was another matter.

I believed that, internally, human beings have real freedom. Yes, of course, we are inevitably products of our family upbringing as well as our culture. That, I took for granted. But human freedom to make real cognitive and emotional choices, to choose to see and feel things differently? I lived my daily life out of the assumption that not only I had this freedom, but that at the very least the people who share my world with me also have it. Why bother otherwise with introspection, reading the paper, therapy, teaching, or talking to your spouse, much less prayer? This led me to admit that I had been sneaking in an opposition between free mind and determined body in a way science itself rejects.

At the same time, I came to see that, if human freedom is real, even if it is very limited, then the old mechanistic model of world as watch and God as distant watchmaker that lay behind my old convictions could not hold. Clock parts almost certainly don't make decisions and thus alter the course of the clock's running; people do. But if this is true, I decided I should not hesitate to claim this same freedom for God and thus be free myself to ask God for what I needed with the expectation that God would, one way or another, be equally free to hear my prayer and take it seriously.

But, this being the case, I was still left with the problem of who I, Roberta Bondi, was with respect to God as I prayed. I couldn't be the small and insignificant subject of an all-knowing, all-powerful king; for me that would never work. Blessedly, scripture and the early monastics finally gave me an answer, or rather God answered my need through them. I could come to God in prayer "as a friend of God."

The notion of friendship with God is fundamental in the early literature on the Christian life. The second-century Irenaeus told me that human beings were created to be companions of God. The *Sayings of the Fathers* of the Egyptian desert described for me Abba Moses' friendship with God, and both the fourth-century Gregory of Nyssa (following his brother Basil) and the fifth-century Theodoret of Cyrrhus depicted friendship with God as the very goal of growth in the Christian life.

The Bible supported them, too. The Old Testament speaks of both

Abraham and Moses as "the friends of God." In the Gospels, Jesus tells us that such friendship is not reserved only for the spiritual elite. Jesus, who in John is nothing if he is not God, tells his disciples in 15:15 that they will no longer be called his servants, but from henceforth he will call them friends. In Jesus' relationship with Mary and Martha and what happened when Lazarus died, we see an illustration of this friendship.

"But," I can hear you saying, "I have been singing 'What a Friend We Have in Jesus' for years, and it hasn't helped my petitionary prayer any. What characteristics of friendship are you talking about here, anyway?"

I believe they are the qualities that characterize any real human friendship. First, friends share the same deep desires. According to Theodoret, "This is the definition of friendship: liking and hating the same things." Theodoret is not talking about superficial likes and dislikes here. He is speaking, rather, of the way in which, in a real friendship, the lives of the friends are so bound together that the well-being of the one depends in a fundamental way on the satisfaction of the deepest desires of the other.

Now, in popular piety we are accustomed to think of God wanting what we want; we need here to think of a characteristic of our friendship with God as longing for what God wants. What does God want? Scripture is plain: God wants the well-being of not just me, but all the people God loves whom God has created. Praying as friends of God, therefore, means not asking just for what we need, but asking, and longing for, the well-being of the people God loves, even those for whom we, left to ourselves, would choose not to care. When I pray "give us this day our daily bread," therefore, I am praying that God will provide for the basic needs of others as well as for my own, and I pray it knowing that God already wants what I ask for far more than I do myself.

Second, friends share with each other what they are thinking and feeling, even if they assume the friend can't or won't respond with more than interest and sympathy. Why should we tell God what we want or need if God already knows it? The question misses the point: there is no way to have a real friendship if we are unwilling to talk over our deepest feelings, fears, and desires with our friend. Without such willingness to talk, friendship—and marriage and family life, too—degenerates into no more than polite acquaintanceship. In terms of our prayer, then, if our relationship with God is to thrive, we have to speak the petitionary prayers we have in our hearts, no matter how worthy or unworthy we think they are or what we might think the outcome may be.

Third, friends hold each other accountable. It is simply not possible to have a friendship where, no matter what the other person does, it is fine with us. Real friends expect a lot from each other in the way of loyalty, care, truthfulness, and faithfulness to the unspoken promises that govern that friendship. Where these expectations are violated, the friendship is threatened until the situation can at least be discussed.

We accept that God holds us accountable in this way without any trouble, but somehow we are inclined to believe that real Christians ought simply to accept whatever happens as "the will of God." This is not, however, what Jesus recommends in the parable of the friend at midnight or the parable of the widow and the unjust judge. We are to push God on God's promises as Moses did when it looked as though God was about to destroy the people of Israel after the incident of the golden calf. Being friends of God means we need to argue as Mary and Martha did in John 11, when they confronted Jesus on his absence at the time of Lazarus's death. What would have happened to their friendship if they had simply responded to Lazarus's death with, "we must be quiet and accept it as the will of the Lord"?

Fourth, friends need each other. I realize the idea that God might need us is alien to much of our teaching that God is beyond need. If we take Jesus seriously, however, when he tells his disciples that "whoever has seen me has seen the Father," then we must also understand the implication that God, for whatever reason, seems to have chosen to need us, and our prayers as part of the foundation of life with God give back something to God that God longs for from us.

All this being the case, why, then, do we sometimes get what we pray for but so often we do not? Sometimes the answer is, no doubt, that what we want isn't good for us, or we ask for too much or even for the wrong thing. More often than not, however, I think there is more to it than this. Human friends, after all, almost never are in a position to give each other everything they want. Hardly anybody's world is so narrow that it revolves around one person alone. Friends have other friends, families, and obligations beyond the limits of a particular friendship, so that satisfying the needs or desires of any one person must always be weighed against the needs and desires of the other people in their lives. If this is true for human beings, however, how much truer must it be for God, who is intimately related to and cares deeply for every person alive?

At the same time, no real friends, no matter how close and loving, ever become so close that they share everything or understand each other perfectly. This is not meant to be a point of regret. Rather, at the core of every human being lies an irreducible otherness, a transcendence which, according to the Cappadocians, is based in God's own transcendence. Friends desire the same things but not all the same things. Every friend has a mysterious life outside the friendship; each friend lives out a trajectory that is uniquely his or her own, and this, too, contributes to why our friends often do not give us what we ask. Again, if this mystery is true for human friendship, it is certainly true of friendship with God. We don't live God's life; we don't understand all God's motivations and especially what limitations God places on God's self for the sake of love of the world.

Yet, in Jesus' prayer he teaches us to ask for what we believe we need. We can be certain that God desires our friendship, and, indeed, created us for this end. It is out of our own love, in response to God's desire for friendship with us, that we pray for ourselves, for each other, and for the world God loves, "give us this day our daily bread."

But what is this "daily bread" we pray for? I don't really believe it is necessary to specify it. As I have said so many times already, and as I still have to remind myself, it is different for different people and even different for the same people at different times. It can also be many things at once.

For the ancient North African Christians to whom Cyprian wrote, it was only for the bare necessities of the day. This was because they and he worried that to pray for—and receive—those things which would appear to provide them with long-term security would make them unprepared to face the martyrdom that could come to them at any moment.

For me, it is often for formation of the heart in love. Security is not always such a good thing as I might want to think it is. Though I have never yet been in a situation where I have been threatened as Cyprian's congregation was, it is surprising how, many times when I have been tied up in knots by my desire for a secure future for myself, my family, my friends, or my community, I have found it helpful to ponder Cyprian's insight and pray, "My God, anxieties over what might happen a year from now are overwhelming me. Help me remember that I actually face the future best, most flexibly, with the most integrity, most in accordance with the actual needs of others and myself, if I can let go of my desire to control what I cannot control so that I can respond appropriately to what actually might happen. For this reason, I ask you now only for our daily bread, for the basic necessities for thriving today."

Sometimes my prayer is not so measured or considered, and then this "daily bread" I ask for is that for which my heart longs, that without which I can hardly imagine my life. Such prayer is extravagant, a truthful expression to God of what I really feel without much consideration for whether what I pray for is for the best. I pray this way because if I don't, I will cut myself off from God or I will burst. Over the last few months I have prayed this way again and again for Melissa's life. I have prayed like this for many things in the past, and I expect to pray in this manner over and over in the future.

Very often, our prayer is for those we do not even know as we remember that when we pray, we always pray as part of God's people. We pray for Christians and for non-Christrians who are in need wherever they may be. We pray for hope, the daily bread for the hopeless, for refugees in camps and refugees driven out of camps, for children in war in danger of massacre, for human beings in ghettos, for the old and forgotten, for the inconsolably grieving, for the sick, especially for those who suffer dreadfully from mental illness. For all of these we pray that God will give them their daily bread by filling their most fundamental needs.

Certainly, as various writers of the early church tell us, the "daily bread," the necessary bread for life we pray for, is often the Eucharist, the very body and blood of Christ, for Jesus himself told us in the Gospel of John, *I am the true bread* and again, *I am the bread that has come down from heaven.* This body and blood of Christ, this bread of our salvation, is our life, our life together and in God. It is healing for our ability to love the Lord our God with all our hearts and minds and strength and souls and our neighbors as ourselves.

And always, right now, my friend, for myself in these days that are so confused, so busy, and yet at the same time so intensely focused on the needs of those I love, I pray for an awareness of the presence of God, which is my daily bread. Though I can struggle through a few weeks with only tastes of it here and there, in the long run how can I live without it?

Write to me soon. Your letters are a gift I ask for. Send me the bread I need that comes with your words and your love. Take care of yourself, my good companion on the way. Give greetings to your folks. Let's pray for each other the best we can.

Roberta

CHAPTER FIVE

My dear friend,

Thank you so much for asking about Melissa, and how I am doing. Everything right now is pretty much as it was. She has just had a good weekend away with her husband at the beach, and her pleasure, of course, helps me. Don't worry; I will keep you up to date. I also want to tell you how much I appreciate your honesty in expressing your questions—and your anger—around the whole matter of praying the petition of Jesus' prayer we've come to now: "forgive us our trespasses as we forgive those who trespass against us." Most of us are too intimidated by the notion that we should find forgiveness easy to begin to be able to tell the truth about how hard we actually find it. I know it's tough to admit that you are having trouble forgiving your own spouse, whom you love so much. I'm hardly surprised that talking to me about it makes you worry that I will not understand how much love there is between you.

I'm glad you asked me whether, apart from my troubles with my father, I have ever had difficulties with praying "forgive us our sins as we forgive those who sin against us" when I am angry at Richard. You say Richard and I have always seemed to you to be so happy together. Could we possibly ever have had anything serious between us that needed forgiveness?

For heaven's sake, my friend, how can you even begin to imagine we wouldn't have had problems that involve forgiveness? Do you actually believe you know any people in a real relationship with each other who haven't? I am fifty-six years old, and Richard and I have been married almost twenty years. Granted that my problems look different from yours, and given that forgiveness is harder for some people than for others, how could I possibly never have had difficulties with forgiveness? Forgiveness of small injuries as well as large is the very stuff of relationships. Of course I find it easy enough to forgive Richard, generally speaking, especially if I don't believe it is going to threaten my being, my image of myself, or my comfort; but to forgive is another matter if I think it is really going to cost me something significant.

I've had trouble with forgiveness—understanding what it is, seeing God's role in it, and doing it—ever since I was a child. I still remember the first time I thought in Sunday school, wrongly I believe, that I had really grasped the import of Jesus' parable of the unforgiving servant. Jesus seemed to be saying to me, God does, indeed, forgive your sins, but God's forgiveness is conditional: if you do not yourself instantly and absolutely forgive those who have injured you, then God will not forgive you in return.

What I understood frightened me witless. As you know, I spent most of my early childhood in a secret, guilty rage over what I considered to be my father's unreasonable authoritarianism and my mother's gross unfairness because of the privileges my brother was given (like not helping with dishes, getting to make noise, and wearing what he wanted) simply because he was a boy, so I knew I was sunk. I believed I could never get over my anger and forgive them, or my brother, either.

As you mentioned in your letter, like you, I also believed that forgiveness means so letting go of an injury that you no longer even consider that you have been hurt. Neither you nor I invented this idea out of our heads, you know. We were both taught that if you forgave someone, you had to say, and mean it, that it was "all right" that the other person had hurt you. Though I wouldn't have been able to put it like this when I was a child, to me, at least, this meant that I was being asked to collude in my own injuries, which I could not do, no matter how hard I tried.

Perhaps you think that I must have been an unusual little girl because this last feeling I describe sounds awfully adult. You may be partly right; I think I was more self-reflective, resentful, and stubborn than a lot of children of that age. I know, nevertheless, that there was nothing unusual in the unreasonable and contradictory things that I believed about Christian forgiveness which still sometimes haunt me. If you don't believe me, let me tell you a story from my childhood which you, and almost everyone else we know, can certainly duplicate in one form or another.

From the time I was little, I had been a shy, daydreaming sort of girl who had a hard time speaking her mind or her feelings, especially with adults, but who expressed herself fairly well through making pictures. About a week before my eighth birthday, my mother asked me what I might particularly like for a birthday present. In fact, I had already thought about it a lot. Apart from soft colored pencils, which my parents had already told me cost too much, what I really wanted, I said, was one of those huge green and yellow boxes of sixty-four crayons.

The next week, even though I was hardly surprised when I unwrapped these very crayons, I was thrilled with my present. All through the evening I opened and closed the box to sniff the new smell of my crayons and admire their flat-topped points. Later that night before I went to bed, I carefully took them out one by one to read the names of the hues which were printed on their paper wrappings.

The next morning, I brought my treasure to Sunday school. Working on a picture of Abraham's sacrifice of Isaac, I gloated as I showed off the crayons to the other children. No one else had a silver crayon like the one I was using for Abraham's knife, or a white, like the one I was about to apply to the fur of the ram caught in the thicket!

My self-satisfaction did not last long. While I worked away with my new crayons, Janey sat next to me. Having forgotten her own crayons, she was forced to color with the Sunday school's beat-up, peeled, and broken crayons from the cigar box that sat on the middle of our low table. Janey, normally the class leader and "teacher's pet," didn't like being in this one-down position, any more than she liked my display.

"Show off!" she leaned over and hissed at me when she thought Mrs. Jason couldn't hear her.

"Am not," I whispered back.

A Place to Pray

"I'll fix you," she replied. Keeping an eye on the teacher, she whipped out her hand, grabbed up my green and orange box, and pulled out my beautiful silver crayon, which I had already made the mistake of telling her was my favorite.

"Bobbie Marie, can I borrow this?" she asked sweetly and loudly. The crayon was already in her hand as she spoke. As I tried my best to grab it back, she pressed my new crayon's point as hard as she could on the picture she was drawing, which was a very mean-looking Goliath in full armor. Of course, my crayon snapped in half.

Shocked and horrified, I burst into tears.

At this point, Mrs. Jason intervened. "Janey," she said, "I saw you do that. Now, tell Bobbie Marie you're sorry."

Smirking slightly in her frilly dress and patent leather shoes, Janey looked down in exaggerated innocence at my remaining crayons, clasped her hands behind her back, and answered in a sing-song, "I'm sorry I broke your crayon, Bobbie Marie." We both knew she didn't mean it.

I stared heartbroken and silently raging into my ruined set of crayons, while the teacher turned to me. "Bobbie Marie," she said, "Janey has just apologized, so now you must tell her it's all right, that you forgive her and will be her friend."

I couldn't say the words; I couldn't even look at the teacher and the other child. I had asked for it, it is true, but my crayons had been my favorite birthday present and they were spoiled. How could I say it was all right when it wasn't? How could I be expected to forgive her?

It was exactly what was expected of me, however. "Bobbie Marie," the teacher prompted, kindly but more firmly. "Jesus tells us that if we want God to forgive us for the things we do wrong, then we have to forgive other people whether we want to or not. Now, Bobbie Marie, what do you have to say to Janey?" She looked at me and waited.

I cleared my throat and tried to answer.

"What was that?" she said.

"I forgive you," I mumbled. I still couldn't look at either of them. I was much too angry and too humiliated ever to want to see either of them again. "It's all right," I choked out at last.

Chapter Five

At that point the teacher heaved a sigh of what I assume now was relief that she had aborted a scene as well as having made her moral point about Christian forgiveness. Chin raised, Janey broke out in a triumphant smile. Apology or not, she knew she had taken me down one peg by ruining my crayons, and down another by making sure I continued to be helplessly angry about it.

As far as I was concerned, the whole exercise in forgiveness was a disaster. Part of me was ashamed of my anger, which made my unforgiveness worse. At the same time, whatever the teacher had told me that Jesus wanted or threatened, I couldn't simply forget that Janey had broken my crayon; even if she had been sorry, my box of crayons would still be ruined. I did not want to be friends. I was also humiliated that I had just let myself be coerced into committing the sin of lying to Janey and the teacher, by saying that what Janey had done was all right.

Does this story sound familiar? If you tell me it doesn't, I won't believe you. As I said already, I imagine we all lived through one version of it or another, if not at church, then at school or at home. I am sure, in fact, that it is the source of an awfully lot of our unhelpful and unrealistic adult beliefs about forgiveness.

First, notice that the teacher, Mrs. Jason, really was trying to teach me that forgiving someone is the same as saying that it is "all right" that someone else has hurt you. Whatever he or she has done, once forgiveness is accomplished, the incident is completely over; you are no longer allowed to be angry, sad, or disappointed. Instead, you will be cheerfully, trustingly back to wherever you were in your relationship before the injury took place.

My friend, there are many situations where such a description of forgiveness applies, but there are plenty where it can't, even if we want it to, and we would be much better off if we would admit it. My broken crayon would not have been restored or my disappointment removed even by a sincere apology (which Janey and I both knew hers wasn't). Furthermore, if Janey breaks my crayon, apologizes, and I say "it's all right," does saying "I'm sorry" make it all right if she immediately afterward breaks another child's crayon? How am I to trust her again if I see this happen, much less like her? Again, if I believe that it is "all right" for someone to hurt me provided they tell me they are sorry afterward, is the moral burden on me to accept the apology, if they repeatedly hurt me in the same way and say they are sorry?

To put this in adult terms, is an abused spouse obliged to say her broken leg or his demolished spirit doesn't matter if the other apologizes? Does the injured person have a Christian obligation to accept back the abuser again and again if the abuser only says "I'm sorry," and believe that it will never happen again? I'm afraid the world is full of women whose pastors, following this logic, have told them that, yes, they must accept their husband's apology, take back the abuser, and love him on top of it.

Now don't misunderstand me: the fact is, in any real relationship, plenty of things happen on a day-to-day basis that can be, and need to be, forgiven in Mrs. Jason's "it's all right now, I've already forgotten it" way. These things happen as a result of occasional carelessness, like breaking a favorite dish or forgetting something at the store or even forgetting an anniversary. There are other things, however, that most of us just can't forgive so easily, even if we would like to: words spoken in an argument that were intended to belittle or hurt, a refusal to take the other person's feelings or concerns seriously because they do not matter to you. Perhaps impossible to forgive in this simple way is a broken trust, a betrayal, habitual emotional neglect, ongoing contempt, or abuse.

This gets me to my second point. Notice that Mrs. Jason assumes that forgiveness is something so easy for Christians to do that even children can do it right on the spot just because they are commanded to. Part of the problem here, of course, may be that Mrs. Jason thinks forgiveness should be easier for children than adults because children are supposed to be innocent and uncomplicated and their problems less serious than those of older folks. (What is a broken crayon, for example, compared to a marriage broken by infidelity?) If she thinks children's problems are small, however, she hasn't paid much attention to real children. Boys and girls are not necessarily all that much simpler than supposedly more complex adults. Did you catch the feelings, motivations, desires, and needs of the two children in this story I've just told? They include, just for a start, pleasure, envy, pride, humiliation, craving for recognition, desire for power over others, greed, anxiety, need for a sense of self, desire to look good, grief, rage, self-righteousness, complacency, secrecy, guilt, and betrayal.

Can all the things wrong here be set right simply by one child's being commanded to forgive the other? Of course they can't. But if this is true for those two children, think how often the so-called adult feelings, needs, and desires in situations in which we try to forgive are at least as complex. We certainly don't make forgiveness easier by pretending that we should be able to make all this complexity go away in an instant just by gritting our teeth and willing it.

Third, notice the role of God in this story of the children. As far as Mrs. Jason is concerned, when it comes to getting me to forgive Janey, God's contribution is that of a frightening policeman whose job it is to enforce the law, or that of a cosmic old-fashioned "father" whose name is invoked as a threat by a mother who controls her offspring with, "If you won't forgive Janey, just you wait until your father comes home, and then you'll be sorry!" Such a way of presenting God is not harmless. It taught you and me early that, far from God being the one who looks at us with compassion and most particularly forgives us, God is just waiting for the chance not to forgive us in turn if our forgiveness is not up to snuff.

For those of us who grew up in a household where the rules were strictly enforced or even extended beyond what we had understood them to cover, so that we rarely felt the forgiveness of our parents, how hard it can be ever to believe in the reality of God's forgiveness!

Yet God does forgive us in this way. Think of the often misunderstood passage from Isaiah I mentioned in an earlier letter, where God's ways are said not to be our ways, just because God forgives so much more thoroughly than we do. Look at the rest of Jesus' teaching that makes the Lord's Prayer clear. Remember, for example, the father's relationship not just to the younger brother in the parable of the prodigal son, but also to the other brother as well. When the older brother refuses to forgive the younger for all that has happened, including what he perceives to be his father's favoritism, it is not the father who casts him off, refusing to forgive him in return: it is his own stubborn pride, self-righteousness, and hurt feelings that refuse to let him forgive—feelings and attitudes that we hope in the months and even years that follow will finally be healed.

Though even our own experience might tell us otherwise, as the ancient teachers say God never writes us off in our struggles.

A soldier asked Abba Mius if God accepted repentance. After the old man had taught him many things he said, "Tell me, my dear, if your cloak is torn, do you throw it away?" He replied, "No, I mend it and use it again." The old man said to him, "If you are so careful about your cloak, will not God be equally careful about [God's] creature?"[1]

Forgiveness of others in hard situations is made harder by the erroneous conviction that God is about to throw us out if we do not instantly forgive. Conversely, it is made far easier by the knowledge that we do not have to be perfect for God to love us, or for the universe to have a place for us.

"Well, yes, of course," I can hear you saying now in your sweetly skeptical way. "You've described some unrealistic and unhelpful ideas we both learned early about forgiveness, and you've reminded me that God doesn't write us off when we have a hard time with forgiveness. You still haven't told me what you think forgiveness is, or how I might go about forgiving in the sort of situation about which I wrote you."

You are right, my friend, I haven't yet said what I think forgiveness is or how to do it. This is because I was convinced that it is very important to clear away what forgiveness isn't before I try to do this much harder task you've set me. Now that I've done that, however, I will tell you what I believe to be the most basic requirements of adult Christian forgiveness as Jesus and the Fathers and Mothers of the ancient Egyptian desert whom I study speak of it.

As I understand them, in all given situations, forgiveness has two necessary elements. The first is that we give up the notion of revenge ("turn

---

1. Mius 3. *The Sayings of the Desert Fathers,* p. 150.

the other cheek"), and the second is that we come to desire the well-being of our injurer ("pray for those who persecute you").

"Really!" I hear you mocking me a little. "Is that all there is to it?"

Yes, my friend, at a minimal level, which is often the best we can do, I think it is. I admit that doing these two things may seem easier than our earlier wrongheaded conviction that forgiveness meant liking and believing someone you cannot like or trust, or deciding that the fact that Uncle Joe abused you as a child is now all right with you. Make no mistake, however. Neither of the elements I'm talking about is as easy as it sounds.

Take the idea of giving up revenge against someone who has knowingly hurt you and is not sorry about it. As you yourself know, it is not hard after a while to give up the fantasy of burning down the house of someone who has unjustly put you out of work by lying about you. Really and truly giving up the hope that he or she will some day lose a job in the same way, and so suffer as you have suffered, however, is much harder. Actually getting to the point where you pray for his or her actual thriving—and mean it—this is truly hard.

It is also not surprising that it is hard. Forgiveness is an important element in the love of God and neighbor into which we are growing. Love as the Fathers and Mothers speak of it is not a single, simple action or emotion we either feel or don't feel at any given moment. Love is a disposition we grow into, or are healed into, or are transformed into by God. It is a way of relating to the world, to God, to others, and to ourselves that includes a combination of actions, habits, ways of seeing and making judgments, as well as feelings.

As is true for the practice of all the other virtues that go together to make up love, forgiveness, both as a character trait and as an act in a situation like this, is hard work. In spite of your and my fantasies of how quick and easy for Christians it ought to be, it generally also takes a long time. "Abba Ammonas said, [in the ancient Christian desert of Egypt] 'I have spent fourteen years in Scetis asking God night and day to grant me the victory over anger.'"[2]

---

2. Ammonas 3, *Sayings,* p. 26.

Ammonas said it to his listeners, the two of us included, not to demoralize us but to hearten us. Learning how to forgive and practicing it, like the mastery of anger, as I just said, takes a long time. I have found that this is just as true of forgiveness in my marriage, in my larger family, and in my other relationships of love as it is in my relationships where I would seemingly not have as much at stake.

Of course, I haven't forgotten that the place where you are most struggling with issues of forgiveness is not with strangers or with things from your childhood, but in your own marriage. Neither has it slipped my mind that you asked me to tell you whether Richard and I have had any problems that needed real forgiving, and if so, how I, at least, actually went about doing my part of it. Having satisfied myself that I've cleared away a lot of erroneous convictions about forgiveness that have caused us both pain over the years, I think I've finally come to the place where I can tell you about a serious issue with which we once had to deal.

In some ways, our problem had its accidental origin in our age difference. As you know, almost twenty years ago when we decided to get married, Richard was in his late twenties and I, ten years older. I was in a new teaching job in the seminary. Having taught for several years before I arrived here, however, I had already been given tenure. Richard, on the other hand, had only begun his own university career several hundred miles away, and he was still writing his dissertation. Compared to my income, his was very small, and it was likely to remain that way for a long time to come. In addition, not having tenure, he also lacked job security.

Emotional security as well as job security was important to me. I had two little children from a previous marriage; the three of us had been in Georgia less than a year. The children, who loved Richard, were traumatized, nevertheless, by the previous year's move, and they were clearly not up to another. Not only I, but Richard, wanted what was best for them. As for me, in spite of my happiness in my love of this man to whom I was about to join my life, I was emotionally battered, exhausted, and depressed by the various things that had accumulated and weighed me down from childhood through the years of my former marriage. Considering my unhappiness in that marriage, I found it frightening enough to take the risk of marrying again. I couldn't make myself also risk giving up teaching in Georgia with no more than the hope of finding something else in another city. It also looked as though Richard would have numerous job possibilities in Atlanta. Under the circumstances, the most sensible thing seemed to be for Richard to quit his far-away job, move to Atlanta, and look for opportunities to teach here.

Of course, people don't always do what is sensible, particularly males who were raised to think that a man cannot be a man unless he is bringing home a paycheck bigger than his wife's. Richard, however, has never been that kind of male. He is, rather, the unusual sort of man who, when all is going as it ought to, is the happiest and the most himself when he is using his intelligence and intuition to take care of the people he loves. It was easy, therefore, for Richard to decide that he wanted to move to Atlanta and see what developed here with respect to a job.

Once we were actually married, Richard could not find a full-time teaching job, though he soon found a part-time position in the seminary where I am. For a while this arrangement suited him very well. In the evening after the other three of us had gone to bed, Richard completed his dissertation, and later wrote an excellent book. Apart from his own teaching, the rest of his daytime and early evening were devoted to care of the children and the household. He enjoyed this work, and it made the combination of my own mothering with full-time teaching possible. He was very good at what he did, and not only from my perspective.

"Mama," Benjamin asked me once in his slow, soft voice when he was about six. We had all been together for two years by then. "Do you think Richard would have married you, even if you hadn't had Grace and me?"

In spite of his apparent satisfaction, I was worried that he could not ultimately find this less than full-time teaching arrangement satisfying to him. I benefited from it emotionally, nevertheless. In those hard years, the children, after all, were not the only ones in need of nurturing. Richard loved me, fussed over me, talked to me, listened to me, made me laugh, beguiled me with his curly-haired, green-eyed good looks, cooked for me, and brought me presents, and in my emotionally sore state I soaked it all up like sunshine after a hard winter. I was grateful for every single thing he did for me and for everything he was, and I loved him extravagantly.

This is the way our life was for six or seven years until the children got old enough to need less from Richard. Around the end of that period, I began to spend a lot of my at-home hours fiercely preoccupied with my writing, and more and more of my weekends traveling to meetings and speaking engagements. About the same time, Richard was offered the chance to add the management of the theological school's bookstore to his part-time teaching.

Short of being given a full-time teaching job, on the surface the addition of the bookstore looked ideal. Richard had a Ph.D. in theological ethics, he liked books, and he knew a lot about them. Unfortunately, it didn't work. Though he continued to enjoy his teaching, he quickly realized that he could not truly enjoy the bookstore. While some of it was interesting and full of good human interaction, much of it he found tedious and unchallenging. Then there was the situation with two employers each trying to get the most for their respective dollars. He soon began to feel overworked in terms of tasks and underutilized in terms of talents, all of which was made worse by the fact that the two parts of what he was now doing added up to a one-and-a-half-time job for relatively little pay. Unhappy or not, even in some ways trapped by his disposition to be helpful, he kept on in this way for almost ten years while Grace grew up and left home, Ben went through most of high school, and I continued to spend even more time teaching, writing, and traveling.

During those years I began to thrive. At the same time, though Richard was still his loving, helpful, and considerate self, at some point he also began to seem withdrawn. He complained increasingly about the bookstore as he lost his springy walk, and he became absentminded and uncharacteristically irritable at home. I didn't know what was wrong, and I would often wake up in a cold sweat, worrying that he no longer wanted to be married to me. On other nights I worried that his spirit was being crushed at work. He could not understand my concern about our marriage, though he agreed that he disliked what he was doing, and that his enthusiasm and even joy in teaching were being undermined by the relentless splitting of his energies. Though I believed him about his work, I couldn't quite believe him about our relationship. There was nothing more I could see to do about the way we were, but I suggested that he think of changing careers entirely so he could have a greater sense of purpose and focus. He put me off snappishly when I pushed, reminding me that the children, though almost grown, still needed our financial help, so we couldn't afford the time and the lost income it would take to re-tool.

It was only immediately after Benjamin went off to college, however, that all of these things around Richard's unhappiness came to a head. The preceding summer had been a hard one for me. Though I knew it was a necessary part of his growing up, I was forlorn at the thought of Ben's leaving home, and in spite of his excitement over college, a large part of Ben, too, was bewildered and sad. Just as significantly, for most of those months in which I was grieving Ben, I was out of contact with and very worried about, my beloved unwell aunt who, I only knew, was continually traveling by car somewhere out West with her daughter's family.

Though I was certainly in no mood to go out of town, three weeks before it was time to drive Ben up to Indiana for college I had to leave for a conference in England. After not hearing from her in months, two days before my plane took off, my aunt telephoned to say that she had fallen on some concrete and hurt her hip. With my aunt on my heart and my only son begging me to stay home with him, I left in great anxiety. The very night I returned two weeks later, my cousin called to tell me that my aunt was in the hospital with an infection in her hip, and she wished and intended to die.

What could I do? I wanted to fly out to her then, but I couldn't; in a week we were leaving to drive Ben, who was now crying every day, up to Indiana. Richard by now was so withdrawn and irritable when I spoke of my worries that I felt unable to talk to him.

Somehow, in the midst of all this we took Ben up to school and got him settled. The next day after we returned, I flew out by myself to be with my aunt, and as she wished, to talk the doctors into unhooking the machines that were keeping her alive. It was an awful trip. I came back one day late to my own teaching, shocked and exhausted from what had gone on with Auntie Ree and what felt like the loss of my son. I was dreadfully in need both of Richard's loving care and the peaceful stability of our familiar house.

Neither of these was I to have. Though it had not registered on me until now, Richard himself was also in a serious crisis. He had awakened one morning to realize how truly unhappy he was. He saw at last that he would never be able to teach full time, he felt hopelessly ensnared by the bookstore, and he was trapped with me in the role that he had assumed over the years at home, that of the calm, steady, and selfless husband. He now knew that he had experienced himself as both invisible and weightless, at school and with me. He panicked. If he were not to disappear altogether, he would have to help himself immediately. He decided that to give himself both literal and metaphorical substance he wanted to begin to lift weights. For this, he explained that day when he met me at the airport as I was returning from my dying aunt's hospital room, he needed to move Benjamin's things out of his room, take over the space himself and put a weight bench in it.

Emotionally wrung out, I could not understand a word he said to me. I was devastated and furious. How could he ask me to give up Ben's room at such a time? I felt betrayed. Where was his customary sympathy in the light of what I had been through all by myself with my aunt and the horrors at the hospital? Didn't he love Benjamin? Desperately, I explained my grief, and my need not to have to feel as though Benjamin's presence was being erased from the house.

In his own desperation, Richard could not understand me in return. He was also devastated and even more furious than I. Although he too had loved my aunt, he seemed to minimize the painfulness of the terribly lonely moral decision I had made in supporting and assisting her death. Of course he loved Benjamin, but how could I fail to see the immediate seriousness of his own need? Why was I always so dramatic, as though only my problems counted? Didn't I understand that children went away to college every day without their mothers falling apart? He, too, felt deeply betrayed. Habitually setting his own needs aside in our marriage, he had taken care of me for years. Now, when he really needed me, I would not support him. Benjamin, after all, had left home and our house was small. Did I expect to preserve his room as a shrine?

Believe me, my friend, this was a difficult time for both of us. Oh, some of our difficulties were solved quickly, it is true. In the weeks that followed, I reluctantly agreed that a weight bench would take over Ben's room. Peace was restored in the household. Still, both of us were so hurt, so sure that we were right, and so angry at each other that healing forgiveness in those months was simply not possible.

One major step forward occurred on Richard's side, however, the following August, at the end of the first year in which Richard had been lifting weights. He decided that since teaching full time wasn't ever going to work out for him, what he would really like to do was to enroll in a clinical training program to become a pastoral counselor. Because Ben was still in college, he would temporarily continue the teaching and the bookstore while he was training. A week after his decision, Richard was admitted to a program and began preparing for his new work.

In the months that followed, though part of me was still angry at him, I was delighted that Richard had found what he wanted to do and had taken action on his own behalf. Doing something he liked for the first time in years, he became far less withdrawn and irritable, and his step began to bounce again.

Another training and weight-lifting year after that, Richard was able to quit the bookstore, and for the first time he was able to think about leaving teaching entirely. His job situation, I believed, had been solved. He now had meaningful work. The anger and pain we both had felt that had centered on the weight bench seemed to have gone away of themselves. Our marriage was restored; we had forgiven each other.

Then, just as I was breathing a sigh of relief, the rest of the crisis hit. At the end of our vacation that same summer, Richard told me one day that we needed to talk. Over a mostly uneaten lunch he explained that he was now happy in his work, but he was not happy with me. He loved me and he wanted to be married to me. On the other hand, though he realized it was his problem at least as much as it was mine, he felt suffocated both by the manic energy I expended when I was writing, and by the dreadful intensity I radiated when I wasn't. He wanted me to know that he could no longer live with his sense that whatever he told me about what was going on with him, I always disregarded what he said and interpreted it in my own terms. At the same time, he was sick and tired of trying to live up to my idealized image of him as perfect. It left him no room of his own and no place to be an ordinary, flawed man.

At first I was so taken aback by his words that I hardly knew what to do; I was angry and very frightened. I had had no idea of any of these complaints. Though I had thought him wonderful (even when mad at him), I had never thought him perfect. Furthermore, I had gotten good and sick of pretending to him over the years that he was the strong, nurturing, and good one of the two of us, because it seemed so important to him that I see him that way. Since it made me feel incompetent and helpless, I had hated pretending this. As for the question of my energy which he experienced so destructively, I could only be amazed and horrified, partly because he had often said it had been my intensity that had drawn him to me in the first place. I could not understand at first what he meant when he said that I habitually discounted his interpretations of what was happening with him in favor of my own. Now it was my turn to panic. I loved him with my whole heart, and he seemed to be telling me that simply being who I was was harming him.

So how did we get through this problem in forgiveness, all sixteen years of it if you start from the beginning of our marriage? We began together by truly wanting to get through it, not walk away from it. Though there had been many times two years previously when we had a hard time trusting each other, and even more times when my experience of men told me that, whatever he said, Richard would ultimately abandon me, I was quite certain that I loved him. Both of us were prepared to work hard to set things right. Neither expected what was before us to be fast, easy, or simple. Though we had not yet identified for ourselves what the specific, individual characteristics of our strands were, both of us well understood how complex the interwoven ropes of anger, fear, demoralization, anxiety, loyalty, pride, admiration, self-delusion, gratitude, self-protectiveness, gentleness, and self-righteousness actually were.

Blessedly, we had agreed from the beginning of our marriage that whenever we had a serious issue, we must talk about it until we understood and solved it. We had broken our own rule about talking around the weight bench. We did not make that mistake again. As truthfully as we could Richard and I endlessly asked each other questions and explained ourselves. Night after night I woke him up at two or three o'clock to talk. He did his best not to withdraw emotionally or to be irritable, and I tried my hardest not to overwhelm him with my intensity. We talked before coffee in the morning, driving to the shopping mall in the car, every place.

Talking in such circumstances is not necessarily easy. Indeed, Evagrius Ponticus, one of the fourth-century Abbas I find particularly helpful, had warned me years ago that the temptation of Christians when they were angry with each other is to tell themselves that Christians don't argue. Rather, they should just go away and forget about their injuries. Abandoning the problem like this, however, said Evagrius, was both destructive to the relationship and destructive to the angry person who would finally be consumed by his or her unresolved anger. Somehow, as unwilling to argue and as tempted to try to let our problem solve itself as we both were, we also knew that Evagrius was right: the future of our marriage depended upon confronting all the things that had put us in this situation in the first place.

Fortunately, in our early years together we had made three commitments to each other about how we would argue that made the talking we now needed to do possible. First, we would never deliberately lie to each other or deliberately conceal the truth. Next, neither of us would ever say anything to the other that was actually intentionally hurtful, no matter how angry we were. Finally, we were committed to talk until each of us understood what had happened and we were both satisfied with where we came out. Though we had not always been able to be faithful to the first and third of these (and so had gotten ourselves into trouble), we had never violated the second. Now, we would be scrupulous.

At the same time, though I could do little to contribute directly to Richard's interior work, I knew that the problems Richard raised were mine at least as much as they were his. For years I had puzzled over such statements in *The Sayings of the Fathers* as "the closer a person comes to God, the more a person knows herself to be a sinner," and "consider yourself lower than the beasts, and know that the beasts are not condemned." I had always hated sayings like these because they seemed to reinforce the preaching on sin I had heard as a child at Pond Fork Baptist Church. There, sin was about my basic contemptibility, unworthiness, and unacceptability to God. Such an emphasis had hurt me greatly as a child and as an adult.

I did not believe that my ancient teachers understood sin in this way, but what, I had wondered, did their sayings mean? Now, in my longing to set right with Richard what was wrong between us, I began to make sense of these and many other things they said. I saw that they had no interest in metaphysical statements on the status of human beings before God. They were not recommending that we grovel in God's presence and say things like "Compared to you, God, I'm not any good, I've never been any good, and I'll never be any good." Their concern in seeing themselves as sinners was the breaking down of walls and the healing of love between human beings that makes forgiveness possible. Forgiveness and the healing of love cannot take place, however, unless a person becomes deeply convinced that, whatever anyone else has done to her or others, she is more like than unlike the injurer. This is not always easy.

> Abba Poemen said, "If [a person] has attained to that which the Apostle speaks of 'to the pure, everything is pure,' . . . he sees himself less than all creatures." The brother said, "How can I deem myself less than a murderer?" The old man said, "When [a person] has really comprehended this saying, if he sees a man committing a murder he says, 'He has only committed this one sin but I commit sins every day.'"[3]

This meant that I must learn to see myself as a sinner with respect to Richard, to give up what in this case was my need for the self-righteous vision of myself as innocently wronged, and to know, deeply, that when it came to harm in our relationship, I myself was on the same side of the fence as Richard, if for no other reason than simply because the two of us were human beings.

During this period, therefore, I used my prayer for intense reflection on the things in myself that had contributed to the unhappy place where we were. Taking several weeks to go back to the beginning of our marriage, in the supporting presence of God, I tried to look truthfully at my part in

---

3. Poemen 97, *Sayings of the Fathers,* p. 180.

the patterns of our marriage (some of which I have already told you), including how I had seen Richard, what I had expected of him, and what I believed he had expected from me. After that, I tried to see how I had let my ways of being with him be governed by my fears that came from a past far different from my present.

Much of what I found was excruciating but enlightening and freeing. For example, there was no doubt that I had loved Richard, cherished him, and enjoyed him. Though I had continued throughout our marriage to marvel at his loving and generous nature, I had never thought that he was perfect or that he needed to be. At the same time, coming to him originally with a terrible vulnerability from a sense of my own unlovableness, and as well as from my fear of being abandoned, I had known that he had felt that he had to be perfect to make up for my previous losses. I had responded over the years, first, by reveling in his care of me, but later, after so many of my wounds were healed and I had become strong, by concealing my relative emotional strength, refusing to push Richard to change his image either of himself or of what I needed and wanted from him.

This failure was a major injury I inflicted on him. True, I had refused to push him because I knew that his positive image of himself depended to an extraordinary extent upon his feeling that he was taking care of me. On the other hand, I could see now in my prayer that my refusal had not stemmed from my protective care of Richard in return. In my own habitual fear, which, considering who my husband is, was completely unrealistic, I did not want to challenge him or to argue because I believed that he would cease to want me if he understood that I no longer totally leaned on him as I once had. Paradoxically, I was convinced that without him I would die.

My discovery of this in myself meant that I could no longer help knowing that by refusing to take on my own fundamental, governing fear, I had failed love. I had injured him by my dishonesty, my lack of trust, and my unholy imagination that had, just as he had complained, taken what he said to me and twisted it into something else. Though I had known that Richard had been unhappy, in my own self-centered terrors, I had assumed that the origin of that unhappiness was my fault. I had thought of Richard as deliberately withdrawn from me, when, in fact, he was seriously depressed.

How could I get through the shame of discoveries like these? First, I realized the truth of Abba Poemen's instruction to Abba Isaac: "Let go of a small part of your righteousness and in a few days you will be at peace."[4] All of a sudden, I found that identifying myself as a sinner, not just along with Richard but with the rest of the world, was freeing and not shaming. Somehow I, among all the rest of the world, had thought that I needed to be a perfect wife and a perfect person in order to have the right to breathe the air. I had tried so hard over the years. Now I understood that the sun really does shine on the just and the unjust, and not because the just makes it shine, either. God loved the person I was: indeed, God gave me my very being; it was not something I had to earn or that Richard could give me or withhold from me, even in the unlikely possibility that he left me.

Beginning to see this about myself, I could start to ease up and listen to what Richard continued to explain to me, about his own needs in general and his needs from me in particular. Knowing myself to be a sinner toward him as he really had been toward me, I was no longer pierced to the heart by what he said. I could grieve for both of us. I could and did apologize to him for not listening to him, for not trusting that he was telling me the truth, for not being honest, for referring everything back to me, and for greatly contributing to his perception of himself as invisible.

I still, however, couldn't make sense of what Richard had said about my difficult, single-minded intensity. Richard and I were different, this is true, but in this respect, at least, though I did believe that I should be more like him, a big part of me was convinced that he was the one who needed to be different. Why, I wondered, didn't he naturally go into himself, as I did, to understand the things that caused him trouble? How could he live so much in the present? How could his interests be so spread out among

---

4. Poemen 141, *Sayings of the Fathers*, p. 187.

so many people, and his energy and attention be so diffuse? I was confused and still hurting from his words.

Then in January, many months after the beginning of our conversations, as I was saying my prayers one morning and wrestling with this particular part of our problem, God gave me some help. As I was sitting quietly without speaking, an image came to me as sharp and clear as green leaves in yellow sunlight. It was of two plants in bloom. One of the two, which I understood was me, was a dandelion whose single yellow blossom lay tenaciously flat against the ground and whose tough single root went without branching straight down into the dark earth ten feet or more. The other, which I knew to be Richard, was a bushy, exuberant chrysanthemum. Its roots were a tangle of hair, short, dense, and diffuse. The part above ground was splendid, luxurious in its notched leaves, and covered with extravagant yellow flowers the very color of the single dandelion.

I sat there on the unmade bed that morning, and until it faded, I contemplated the image of these plants with joy. I understood now that I had believed that there was only one right way to be: Richard's way or mine. If Richard could not live with me, I suspected mine must be the one that was wrong, and yet I was very resentful about it. Richard, conversely, seemed to have felt something similar about me. What I had been shown, however, was so obvious it was hard to imagine how either of us could have missed it. We were different plants, different species. One of us was a dandelion, whose strength is its taproot; one a chrysanthemum, whose strength is its bushy life above ground. We were two very different plants growing together, neither better than the other.

Oddly, my friend, it was this knowledge, I think, that after three years of consciously struggling enabled me to complete my own part of the work of forgiveness I needed to do. Not surprisingly, as the Fathers and Mothers warn, we do still need to fight against much of what originally plagued us and made each of us harm the other. For my part I suppose I will always struggle with a fear of abandonment, but I no longer have fantasies of his leaving. I am much more able to accept that both of us make mistakes, and that the worth of neither of us to God or to each other depends upon our getting things right all the time. I really do think I understand what happened around the weight bench, what the needs of each of us were, and why we were not able to respond to each other's needs. I practice being truthful, speaking up, and trusting our relationship. I work at giving up the need to try to control the future. I certainly no longer experience Richard as withdrawn. In fact, as such things often do, the work we did together in the arena of our relationship helped him resolve his attitudes toward meaningful work. He began to see he had actually traded the invisibility and lack of focus he had despised on one level for the false haven of not having to accept and deploy fully his own power in the world: his fear of my intensity was partly a reluctance to accept his own. I am happy to say he recently resigned from institutional teaching and has well begun a career as pastoral counselor and workshop leader. He is present in his life and present to me in a way I've never known him to be before. I hope for another thirty years or more together.

It is in the memory of all that I have just told you that I pray each day "forgive us our sins as we forgive those who sin against us." "Loving, generous, and ever forgiving God, I thank you for the gift of forgiveness, for what you give to me from yourself, and for what you enable me to offer. Help me remember that I am a sinner and, when it comes to the business of learning how to forgive and love the people I will encounter today—Richard, my students, the person who gives me a hard time in the grocery store—this is good news. Please forgive what I cannot yet do myself. I ask these things in your own name, my God, you who in your love have promised to forgive us everything."

Dear friend, I hope in all of what I have described you may find something helpful for your own work. Let me know what you think, particularly whether there has been something of benefit for you in what I have gleaned from the Gospels and from my good teachers of the early church. Remember especially their comforting warning that forgiveness takes a long time.

Take care of yourself, my friend.

With love,
Roberta

CHAPTER SIX

My dear friend,

Please forgive me for waiting such a long time to respond to your last letter. Things haven't been smooth for Melissa over the last few weeks. She has begun the stem-cell therapy. Theoretically, at least, everything is going as it ought. Technically, her body is responding "appropriately"— though how they can tell that is beyond me, considering how experimental it all is. Her chemically induced symptoms certainly wouldn't suggest it: this time when her white count was so low from all the poisons in her system, she came down with an infection that left her with a throat so sore she was unable to swallow or even speak. She ended up on very strong morphine in the hospital from Friday through Monday the weekend before last. Remembering almost nothing of the experience, she came home still too weak to walk or eat. She began to recover a few days later only to be knocked down again by horrible depression from which she is just now beginning to recover.

Considering my present feelings, sorrow, and frustration at my own helplessness, now is probably not the right time for me to be reflecting with you on "lead us not into temptation but deliver us from evil." My mood is bad. The rational part of me knows very well that Melissa's cancer is really not evil, nor are the terrible treatments Melissa is receiving. At the same time, another part of me, which is not open to common sense, finds it impossible simply to say, "Cancer is a natural part of life, neither good nor bad, and of course, the awful poisons she is being given are actually intended for her welfare."

As for thinking about Melissa and the question of temptation, I'm also having a hard time disregarding the way people back away from me in fear or distaste when I mention her cancer. This doesn't bother me nearly as much, however, as the occasional Christian who will respond, "Yes, things look bad right now, but remember Paul's words, 'God will not let her be tempted beyond her strength.'" Does the person who would say such a thing think that Paul means, "If she is a person of faith, then God will not allow her to endure so much physical or mental suffering that she breaks?"

I just can't get over how unrealistic, inadvertently judgmental, and wounding this Christian platitude sounds right now, no matter how good the intention behind it. I am not only thinking of Melissa's treatment-induced deep depression of the weekend, but of all the other sufferers who do seem to break under their pain. What about the folk driven by mental illness to commit one form of suicide or another when their anguish becomes unbearable? What of women raped in war, women whose families and villages will no longer allow them to live in their old homes? Is their faith defective if they can't bear it? What of fathers and mothers who helplessly watch their sons and daughters destroy themselves with alcohol or drugs, of parents who must watch the esteem of their beloved children eroded by racism, of girls and boys abused by those who are supposed to care for them, of old people dying utterly alone, unwanted and uncared for?

I recall a friend of mine who is an Armenian Orthodox priest telling me about a trip he took to Armenia after that dreadful earthquake a few years ago. I can never forget the description of his forays, night after night, into the streets of the little town in which he was staying. At two and three o'clock in the morning the roads were crowded with crazily clad men unable to sleep. They walked and walked among the rubble of their former houses, silently grieving their lost children, their missing wives and parents. Of course, it is possible to say that, since they are still on their feet, God has not allowed them to reach the breaking point, but this is only quibbling, as far as I am concerned. And it strikes me as unspeakable arrogance to assume that those who could not even walk but lay staring vacantly on the ground were demonstrating that they had not been people of faith to begin with.

Even some of the ancient Christian martyrs who survived the persecutions knew not to make this judgment on their fellows who had given in under torture. There is so much that even Christians find themselves unable to endure, and none of us can know how we might bear it. Who is to say what it is that enables one person to hold on and another to give up in despair?

So why do so many of us want to quote—and hear—this verse about God not sending us more than we can bear? When I can fight my own very real temptation to be judgmental toward others who seem to me to be so judgmental, I imagine that it is because it gives us easily frightened human beings a way to redescribe how unspeakably awful some things are which human beings have to face in the ordinary course of life. Quoting Paul's verse is a talisman against being destroyed by the vision of suffering; it suggests that we don't have to be afraid for ourselves because whatever happens, we can know it will not be too much for us.

Though it sets the sufferer at a distance, and incidentally destroys love—the opposite of our Christian goal—our need to explain away another person's pain can sometimes seem almost innocent. Yet it occurs to me, my friend, that if we do redescribe the suffering of others in this way, we certainly can't use Jesus as our authority. Jesus, after all, shared with us in real human life. That is why he cried out from the cross where he felt utterly abandoned, "My God, my God, why have you forsaken me?"

Now, I know, as you are reminding me, that many ancient teachers and modern scholars claim that the cry of Jesus is not one of despair, but rather only a quotation from the first part of a psalm that otherwise has a happy ending. As for me, I'm afraid I'll never be able to accept such a watering down and taming of Jesus' words. What I hear—what I need to hear—is the sob of anguish in the mouth of a dying human being who shared our human lot. It is a great comfort to me to know that it was in this very man—not *in spite of* his suffering, but *in* his suffering—in whom Christians claim God fully dwelt.

The truth, after all, as I said in an earlier letter, and as I need to keep reminding myself now, isn't that Christians are expected or even able to live fully at this very moment in the Kingdom. When we can partly inhabit it, or sporadically dwell in it, that is a great gift for which we must be grateful. Still, in this world life in the Kingdom must always be incomplete. The pain that comes with being mortal is dreadfully real, and if we are to live as free of the fear of such pain as we can, then we must be truthful about it.

Now, my friend, having been able to get all this off my chest, I think I am ready to begin. As usual, thank you for listening to me. Right now it is only knowing that you take me seriously that enables me to think through how I might pray "lead us not into temptation, but deliver us from evil" in such a way that, rather than provoking a tirade of anger from me, Jesus' words might help me grow in love of God and neighbor. What would any of us do, I wonder, without our friends?

So to our considerations. Let me start with a problem with Jesus' prayer that has always bothered me; it is the word "lead." How could Jesus tell us to ask God not to *lead* us into temptation? Even as a child it worried me to think of God as the source of temptations. Was Jesus meaning to suggest that it is God who entices us to do harm? Did God provoke my brother to make faces at me, or goad the owner of the drugstore to lay out such attractive jawbreakers by the cash register that I would sneak out and buy the forbidden candy with the allowance I was supposed to be saving?

Well, of course not, I hear you say. Don't you know that the Greek word we customarily translate "temptation" does not mean "temptation" at all, but rather, "testing"?

Yes, of course I do, but I have to say that I am no happier with the idea of God testing people than I am with the idea of God enticing folk to sin. As an explanation of why terrible things happen to people like Job and his children, the notion of being tested by God may have made sense to the ancient world, but it doesn't suit me, nor does the idea that God *allows*

"Satan" or anybody else to test us. I still find the whole notion repulsive and unworthy of God.

Let me illustrate what I mean with an analogy from human relationships. Imagine that Joe, an acquaintance of mine, has invited me to his party. Once I am there, I almost immediately spy Sally, a woman whom I have not seen for a few months. I am very glad to see her. I know that she once had a terrible problem with alcohol; tonight she looks wonderful. We begin to talk. Sally makes a joke about hard liquor, and I respond that it has been a long time since drinking controlled her life.

"You're right about that," says Sally. "I've been working the Alcoholics Anonymous program for five years now," she goes on, and she begins to tell me how it happened that she began attending it.

Of course, I'm grateful for the chance to hear her story, and I smile back at her.

At this point Joe, our host, walks up, a fresh drink in his hand. From the way he looks, he has already had a bit more than was strictly good for him.

He greets me, then sneering, he turns to Sally. It is immediately obvious that he has heard the last part of our conversation. "I can't stand all these self-help groups people keep joining," he says to her. "It is just narcissism, you know. All they are doing is reinforcing each other's wishful thinking."

Here Sally interrupts. "Joe," she says, "whatever else A.A. is, it is not wishful thinking; it is hard work. Surely you know that."

"Sure, sure," Joe replies, snidely; "anything you say. I'll bet if I put this drink in your hand, you can't stand here for ten minutes without swallowing it." He looks Sally up and down and raises one corner of his mouth in the imitation of a smile.

Sally shifts from one foot to the other. Sweat begins to slick her throat above the neckline of her good black dress and runs down her skin around her pearls. She puts her pocketbook over her shoulder and clasps her hands behind her back. She doesn't answer her host, but she swallows three or four times.

Joe, unsatisfied by her silent response, will not give it up. "Come on," he says, "if you can keep that drink out of your mouth, I'll buy you a steak dinner any time you choose." He laughs and slaps her on the back with his empty hand. "You don't even have to eat your steak with me. See that woman in the blue dress in the corner? I'm going to go talk to her. In ten minutes I'll come back and see how strong you and your A.A. buddies really are. What about it?" Joe raises the other corner of his mouth and looks at Sally expectantly.

Sally keeps her eyes on the floor and twists her purse on its strap as she struggles to find an answer.

"Come on," Joe says again; "take the glass." He thrusts the drink under her nose at the same time he seizes her hand and tries to put the glass in it.

Sally pulls away, but she has been so humiliated and enraged by Joe that it is not at all clear she will be able to resist his dare.

At this point, I intervene. "Joe," I say, "what do you think you are doing? I don't care if this is your house. Now, bug off and leave Sally alone before I make a scene."

Joe turns toward me in a rage. "What's wrong with you, you meddling old woman?" he says. He snatches the glass back, spilling whiskey and water down the front of his expensive pin-striped suit. "This isn't any business of yours, anyway."

Sally straightens up and returns his look. "No thanks, Joe," she says. She has finally understood that she doesn't have to take his dare.

So what about it? Could we think that God deliberately tests us as Joe tested Sally? The author of the Letter of James doesn't think so: "No one, when tempted," he writes, "should say, 'I am being tempted by God'; for God cannot be tempted by evil and [God] tempts no one" (James 1:13). Even if I want to take James's word for it, however, I still find it helpful to look at what Joe seems to be doing with his testing. Joe is exercising power over Sally. He is "putting her in her place." Whether or not he is deliberately malicious in what he is about, Joe wants to portray himself as strong, someone to be feared, by getting Sally to display and acknowledge her weakness before him.

Now my friend, in spite of what James says, you know as well as I that there are plenty of people who do think God tests us like this; moreover, there are many places in the Christian tradition that hint that this is exactly the way God treats us because God does not want us to be in any doubt about our helplessness in the face of God's power.

I, however, can never accept such a picture of God. If it is true that "the one who has seen [Jesus] has seen the Father," then this is simply not what we see in Jesus. Nor is such a need for power visible in the God of the Abbas and Ammas of the desert, or of Athanasius, or of Dorotheos of Gaza, or of Julian of Norwich, or of Gertrude the Great. Neither is it in the loving, generous God I know from the experience of my own life and prayer.

"Well, yes," I can hear you saying, playing devil's advocate. "I agree that Jesus doesn't paint a picture of a God who acts like this, but God is, after all, said to test people in the Bible. Think of Abraham and Isaac, for example. I know, of course, that scripture often describes Satan as the one who is doing the actual tempting and not God. Still, you must admit that in these cases, Satan only does his dirty work with God's permission. Remember Jesus in the wilderness, as well as what happens in the book of Job."

My friend, as far as I am concerned, blaming this kind of temptation or testing on "Satan" (however you want to conceive of Satan) doesn't let God off the hook at all. Would I have had no responsibility for it if I had just stood there without intervening as Joe taunted Sally to her destruction? Of course I would have, and God would have to bear major responsibility for it, too, if God stood by passively as "Satan" worked us over in this way.

"It doesn't matter how you argue," I imagine you answering me in return. "The temptation of Jesus and the story of Job are both in the Bible. What are we to do with that?" Now I can see you frowning with concentration as you think about it. "Doesn't 2 Timothy say that 'all scripture is inspired by God and is useful for teaching, for reproof . . . for training in righteousness, so that everyone who belongs to God may be proficient, equipped for every good work'? If we really believe this, what are we going to do with scripture where it presents us with this sort of problem? I don't think we want to get into a position where we just pick and choose what suits us and discard the rest."

Oh, my friend, how simple life would be if only it were possible to take the Bible and believe everything in it just as it stands! But you yourself know, as much as I do, that this isn't a possibility. One of the gifts and curses of modern biblical scholarship is our new awareness of the way in which the Bible was actually put together: we know now that the words of the Bible come from a span of time that stretches over not just centuries but a millennium or more. The Old Testament alone contains material from the days when the people of Israel were still nomads; from many years later, when they had settled in the land of Canaan; from later still, once they had gone into exile; and even beyond that, when some of them returned to Palestine again to rebuild Jerusalem and resettle the land. As the sources of the Bible are so varied, not surprisingly, many genuinely different, often self-contradictory ways of understanding God appear in its pages, too.

Even folk in the early church knew they could not take the Bible at face value. The ancient Christian teachers were too aware of all the conflicting, often unedifying images of God, the mutually contradictory laws, the odd repetitions in strange places, even the exhortations to what they considered to be immoral ever to believe that they could take the Bible and swallow it down whole. Considering all the different ways the various Gnostic groups alone found to interpret many passages, they couldn't afford this luxury.

So what are we to do with it all? We can't follow the early church entirely: whatever apparent inconsistencies and unsuitable material appeared to lie on the surface, underneath they believed that the Bible had to be consistent with itself because the God who is revealed in Scripture does not change. For our part, though God may not change, we cannot set aside the fact that, inspired or not, the Bible simply presents too many views from too long a span of time to give us a single image of God. We take for granted that revelation comes clothed with the insights and limitations of the human culture through whom the Holy Spirit speaks. The Bible is full not just of offensive images and difficult laws, such as those regulating garments made of cloth woven of two different substances, but also of what often strikes the modern reader as positively immoral: support of slavery, polygamy, human sacrifice, oppression of women, monarchy, anti-Semitism, even the idea that men are saved by faith while women are saved by bearing children.

If all this is true (and if we are honest we can hardly deny it), if we are not only to understand its origins and original intent but actually to be "equipped for every good work" by the reading of scripture, then we must find another way to read it that does so equip us. How we do this is a real problem and a delicate one, too—one whose solution, I'm afraid, can't simply be reduced to the set of rules we would probably all like to have.

At the same time, though I have no intention of giving up my modern knowledge of scripture (as though I had a choice), the ancient teachers I study have gradually also convinced me over the years that when it comes to praying scripture, to reading it as the book of God and God's people, Christians do need to pray the whole of scripture as though it is to be understood through a single interpretive lens. That lens is the person of Jesus. This means that, whatever the original intent of the author, when it comes to praying a particular passage or being "upbuilt in the Christian life," what is inconsistent with Jesus' person and teaching must not be taken literally and certainly not normatively.

When the psalmist in Psalm 137 asks, for example, that God bash the heads of his enemies' babies on the rocks—on the surface a repulsive and cruel prayer—we look at Jesus, who said both "permit the little children to come to me, and do not forbid them," and "pray for your enemies; bless those who curse you." If this is what Jesus taught about children and enemies, then God must feel this way about children and enemies, too. If this is so, however, then the psalmist's words cannot possibly be prayed as they stand. We must speak them allegorically or metaphorically—in the case of this psalm, such writers as Origen in the third century tell us, we are to understand that the heads of the babies we ask God to destroy are actually the first signs of destructive impulses that spring up in us, impulses that have not yet had a chance to grow to maturity.

When I read scripture in this way, I am not simply an individual throwback to the early church. In church history and in actual church life today we find allegorical interpretations of scripture everywhere, whether we acknowledge it or not. From the time I was a child I learned in Sunday school to hear the story of Jacob wrestling with the angel as a story about myself and God, the story of Abraham leaving Ur as an exhortation to courage in taking risks, the story of the water struck from Moses' rock as a promise of help in impossible places. As an adult, the hymns I sing continue to encourage me to identify Jesus as the shepherd of Psalm 23, Christ as the "solid rock" which is the foundation of my life, and so forth. Thus, when I read allegorically passages like the offensive verse from Psalm 137:9, as well as many others that describe God as a warrior or are otherwise full of violence, I do not feel the need to apologize when I ask God to fight vigorously with me against my internal enemies that undermine me or tempt me to self-destruction or the destruction of others.

As for the claim in Timothy that all scripture is inspired by God and of use to Christians, finally, I'm afraid that I do find passages that I cannot read, even metaphorically. I can't help believing that a good many passages in the Bible are edifying only because they are offensive enough, particular enough to an ancient culture, or alien enough to who Jesus is, to force me to think through how I best can answer God's call to growth in love of God and neighbor. This is the way I find I have to read such passages as those referring to slavery and anti-Semitism, or those intending to regulate relationships between men and women, or the many laws and precepts governing acceptable and unacceptable sexual behavior.

Of course there are problems with this approach. For one thing, it doesn't appear to acknowledge that, if Jesus is to be the interpretive lens for scripture, Christians over the centuries have understood Jesus in a whole variety of ways. This, however, is a problem that, as far as I can see, simply cannot be avoided no matter what our theological position. How can our own ways of knowing God in Jesus ever be free of the influences of who we are, both broadly and narrowly? Even if we don't care to acknowledge it, when we encounter Jesus we always do it in the presence of the knowledge, wisdom, and insight of the Christian community which through the ages has tried to pass on faithfully what it has received. We draw on our experience; we read scripture carefully both in the context of study and with the necessary help of the Holy Spirit in the context of prayer; we talk over with friends what we are learning and struggling with, as you and I do, but, wherever we come out, what we know is always conditional. We can never have the luxury of saying "I have discovered the one and only absolute truth."

On the other hand, this way of reading takes very seriously the notion that scripture is not a book of the past but the book of God's people in the present. It expresses understanding that the Bible cannot do its work without the help of the Holy Spirit, who enlivens and raises up both the church and individuals, and the trust that God will speak through scripture in the way we most need to hear it if we are prepared to listen.

Then again, this approach allows me, at least, to make a distinction between what I do when I pray scripture and what I do when I study it to discover its meaning to its original hearers. It gives me a way to acknowledge that the Bible is both the book of God and a human book, which necessarily must refract God's revelation through a particular cultural, historical, human-made lens. It lets it be what it is in the ancient everyday world, while it also lets it be my book and the book of my Christian community through which God speaks.

So, then, am I only reading the Bible "subjectively," finding what I want to find in it according to my own whim? No, but neither do I find in it one single fixed truth that speaks in the same way to all people in all times. If I approach scripture with the help of the Holy Spirit in this way, sure that the word of God is in a real sense inexhaustible, and that no one, and no community, is able to grasp everything in it, and if I bring with me the faith of a teachable heart, as Clement of Alexandria would say,[1] I must expect that God will come to each of us in blessedly different ways according to our need. To read scripture like this isn't straightforward and neat, since God cannot be reduced to a set of universal principles that can be applied tidily to the reading of scripture, but I'm not sure we have any other choice, do we?

All this reflecting on a way of praying scripture does little to answer the question of where temptation might arise and where it is from if it isn't sent in some literal, straightforward fashion by God or "Satan." Fortunately, this is where we can find some real help in what the ancient Egyptian teachers have to say. That they should be able to help us is hardly surprising, of course, considering how great the concern of both the disciples and the Ammas and Abbas was to understand the origin and nature of the temptations. Indeed, from reading the *Sayings of the Fathers,* it is not hard to get the impression that, for many of them, fighting the things that tempted them away from the love of neighbor and God as well as from the disciplines of the monastic life was central to what they were about in the desert.

Where did they think their temptations came from? Beginners to the monastic life, suffering under the unwanted, overwhelming, unrelenting power of their anger, say, or their sexuality or even a desire for a trip into town, were inclined to blame them on the attacks of demons. The Abbas and Ammas who were their teachers, however, steadfastly warned against the desire to lay the blame for their temptations outside themselves.

While acknowledging that demons did go after a few superhero monks (everyone, after all, believed in the malevolent existence of demons in those days), Abba Poemen, for one, was far more interested in getting those around him to recognize that the actual origins of their (our) individual temptations are rarely external to us at all. Rather, they lie in the internal processes, desires, and choices of the particular men and women who endure them.

---

1. *Stromateis,* Bk. I.

Abraham, the disciple of Abba Agathon, questioned Abba Poemen saying, "How do the demons fight against me?" Abba Poemen said to him, "The demons fight against you? They do not fight against us at all as long as we are doing our own will. For our own wills become the demons, and it is these which attack us in order that we may fulfill them. But if you want to see who the demons really fight against, it is against Moses and those who are like him."[2]

As much as we may not want to admit it, according to Poemen and the tradition he represents, no matter how alien, how unwanted we experience our temptations to be, none of them, whether they call forth in us anger, gluttony, inappropriate sexual behavior, anxiety, or fear, would have any power over us at all if they did not already have a home in us in the first place. So much for the old argument that blames women for the unwanted sexual advances of men who do not want to take responsibility for their behavior!

So far, my friend, I would imagine I've told you nothing of their teachings that we modern folk, accustomed as we are to thinking in psychological categories, would regard as particularly noteworthy. What I find surprising, however, is the care they take to ensure that we realize not only that it is we ourselves who are the source of our own temptations but that these temptations we suffer are not in themselves evil. Indeed, according to the Abbas and Ammas, they are a part of the Christian life which we should never expect to go away. As Anthony is recorded as having put it to Poemen, "This is the great work of a [human being]: always to take the blame for his own sins before God and to expect temptation to his [or her] last breath."[3] Or, as another Abba once suggested to his disciple who was struggling with sexual temptation: everybody is tempted; the only reason you would not be suffering from it is that you have already given in to it!

But that temptation is part of the human condition and thus not evil in itself is not the only odd idea that the Ammas and Abbas have to teach. Even

2. Poemen, 67, p. 176.
3. Anthony 4, p. 2.

A Place to Pray

more surprising to me, still, is their insistence that temptations are actually good and useful to the monk trying to grow in love of God and neighbor. By extension, of course, these ancient teachers are suggesting that they are good for us, too. This is why the great Anthony could state quite plainly, "Whoever has not experienced temptation cannot enter into the Kingdom of Heaven." He even added, "Without temptation no-one can be saved."[4]

"Without temptation no-one can be saved!" I don't know about you, my friend, but I really do find this an amazing idea. After fighting my own continual battles against judgmentalism, self-righteousness, stubbornness, neglectfulness, callousness, resentment, laziness, cynicism, fear of abandonment, and despair, the notion that my actual salvation might depend on my experience of these temptations is absolutely mind-boggling.

What on earth are the Abbas and Ammas talking about? It was important to me to begin by noticing that when they speak of being saved by temptations, these teachers assume that these are not just any temptations, but those to which we are not giving in. That is, they are temptations, to anger, judgmentalism, and all the rest, which we are actively attending to and fighting against. Certainly the Abbas and Ammas are not recommending anything so stupid as deliberately putting ourselves in tempting situations to test our endurance.

Rather, the Ammas and Abbas would teach us that what saves us is neither the lack of a particular temptation nor its presence, but the *awareness of our vulnerability* both to the individual, particular temptation that seizes us, and to temptation itself. This is what Abba Poemen meant when he said, "Vigilance, self-knowledge and discernment; these are the guides of the soul."[5] For our ancient teachers, daily attention to and understanding of what is happening within us is fundamentally necessary if we are to grow into the love of neighbor to which we are called. If we are attentive to them, one of the great gifts of our temptations is the glimpse they give us into our own motivations, desires, impulses, and dispositions that are otherwise hidden from us so that we can seek healing.

---

4. Anthony 5, p. 2.
5. Poemen 35, p. 172.

Equally important, however, is the fundamental insight the real, heart knowledge of our own vulnerability to temptation in general gives us into our kinship with other people. This is the knowledge that enables us to realize that as Christians we can never honestly set ourselves self-righteously apart from any other human being, saying, "The sins of this person are so unimaginable that he or she has forfeited any claim to my love or to God's."

If the Abbas and Ammas are right, however, this means that none of us can ever look at someone else's sin or even crime and say, "I would never do anything like that!" This is not just a hard teaching for us; it was hard in the desert, too. I actually quoted this passage to you in my last letter, but I think it is so helpful, let me tell it to you again.

> Abba Poemen said, "If a man has attained to that which the Apostle speaks of 'to the pure, everything is pure' (Titus 1.15) he sees himself less than all creatures." The brother [who was asking him questions] said, "How can I deem myself less than a murderer?" The old man said, "When a man has really comprehended this saying, if he sees a man committing a murder he says, 'He has only committed this one sin but I commit sins every day.'"

The implication here is that if we are to learn compassion—a fundamental disposition if we are to love our neighbor—then we must be able to see, not how we differ from others from whom we would separate ourselves, but how we are similar. It is our temptations that let us see this.

If you are inclined to doubt the truth of this, my friend, let me give you one particularly painful example from my own life. As you know, I have always liked to think of myself as the sort of person who is kind, open, and generous, a nonjudgmental sort who consistently looks with compassion at other people's failures as I wish them to look at mine. At least, I am embarrassed to say, this is the untruthful but wishful view of myself to which I am always tempted, especially on days when I am not paying much attention to what is going on inside me.

Fortunately for my complacency as well as my self-deception, I belong to a book group with which I get together every two weeks. There I regularly find myself in the presence of a man named George, who in the past has been able not only to irritate me but even to enrage me, sometimes simply by sitting in the same room with me. True, I am not the only one for whom George can be a difficult person. He was and still is aggravating in our discussions to the extreme. He interrupts, he tries to co-opt whatever else is going on to his own needs, he insists on talking when the rest of us have agreed to silence, he whines to get his way, and though he inadvertently insults other people constantly he is easily offended. He is also mentally ill, lives by himself in a single room, and is very unhappy.

Now, my friend, being this wonderfully accepting person I like to think of myself as being, you would think that my knowledge of his illness, poverty, and unhappiness would have made it easy for me to be not just tolerant of him but actually to look on him with compassion. Yet, my friend, until quite recently, except for a few unexpected moments, it almost never did. In spite of what I knew, I was frequently tempted sorely to lose my temper with him, I was constantly tempted to push him away from me in disgust, and I was nearly always tempted to shut him up when he was making one of his speeches.

Now, the fact is that almost nothing in my life has been any more helpful to me for seeing into and acknowledging my own self-deception than being around George. During the whole of the time I have known him, my awareness of my own temptations to impatient superiority and contempt have shone the light of Christ into depths of my self-deceptive complacency continually. True, I love my friends, my family, and my students pretty well in the ways I want to love them. Still, how can I possibly tell myself that I am kind enough or understanding enough or, certainly, as compassionate as I need to be in a world of hurt when I am not even able to tolerate what is, after all, the minor irritation of a person who cannot help being irritating and who certainly means no harm? When I see this in myself, how can I maintain a sense of my own innocent acceptance of others?

Without a knowledge of the presence in myself of these love-preventing ways of being, thinking, and feeling, how could I ever learn to love? My temptations with respect to George have helped and continue to help me identify only too easily the exact places where I have needed to work, in my prayer, in my self-reflection, and in my actual relationship with George, if I am to learn to identify with him, feel compassion for him, and to love him.

Certainly I have had to work. Right up till the middle of this last summer, the most useful part of this work included not only praying for him, but also spending a fair amount of time in the presence of God considering in embarrassing detail the things in myself that make me similar to George—my fears and my arrogance, my need to control conversations, my desire to be right, even my occasional almost crazy touchiness. Not surprisingly, such self-reflection did help me, not so much to like George as to be able to start looking on George with compassion. *Very* surprisingly, it also helped me begin to extend the same compassion to myself as I recognized these traits in me.

But temptations are often too much for us without God's help. Certainly, I needed more than what I could do on my own if I were actually to get enough on top of all of what I was struggling with with respect to George, not just to have compassion for him but to begin to love him. God's help came to me one night last summer in the form of a dream.

The dream took place on a hot, rainy Thursday night after one of the meetings of my book group, during which George had been even more out of hand than usual, and I had had to face the fact that I had not made as much progress with respect to my feelings toward him as I had previously thought. I came home demoralized, wet, and angry, and when Richard asked me what had happened at the meeting to make me so out of sorts, I was simply unable to talk about it. I went to bed by myself, sweating and early. After a quick prayer, I fell asleep; almost immediately I had this dream.

I dreamed that Richard and I were together in a far-off city attending a very noisy, crowded book conference in an enormous, confusing classroom building adjacent to a large hospital where we were staying. As the dream opened, we were walking down the hall of the building. Though I was glad to be with Richard, because of the noise, the number of people jammed together, and the lack of oxygen, I was suffering from both claustrophobia and mental confusion. As a result, I was hanging on to Richard's arm with all my might.

We banged our way through the crowds, stopping every few minutes to read notices on doors and look at displays until I could stand it no longer. "Let's get out of here," I said to Richard.

Richard turned to me with surprise. "Not yet," he answered. "You'll be all right. I just need to step into this room and find out what is going on. Don't worry, I'll catch up with you." With that, Richard disappeared into a large auditorium next to us. I was left desperately wandering up and down in a hall full of strangers, more claustrophobic than ever, wondering how I would ever meet up with Richard again.

Then, just as my panic reached epic proportions, I bumped squarely into the chest of a very large man who was coming from the opposite direction. When I drew back and looked up to apologize, I saw that it was George. *Oh no,* I said to myself in dismay. *Surely not George.*

George, however, did not seem to notice my reaction. Instead, he bent down from his considerable height, looked me in the face, and spoke to me. "Oh, Roberta," he said in the kindest of tones, his eyes and mouth conveying nothing but concern for me; "you look so worried. Please tell me what is wrong and let me help you."

And do you know, my friend, surprised as I was by this side of him I never had seen, in my dream I did exactly this. I set aside my pride and my coldness toward him, and I told him in detail of my anxieties and my fear of losing Richard. I let him know how helpless I felt and how angry I was that I didn't know what to do. The whole time I talked, he continued to listen to me with care and gentleness.

When I finished, he spoke words of real comfort and support, assured me that I had not been abandoned, and reminded me that Richard would be certain to look for me in our room if he could find me nowhere else. As he continued to talk to me in the same calm, attentive way, my panic receded until at last, with a few loving pats, he sent me on my way.

My friend, do you know, when I woke up, I was full of the most profound gratitude for the goodness and kindness with which George in my dream returned my own previous unkindnesses. I was also grateful to God who, I was quite sure, had sent me an insight into George's very real, though well-hidden, innocent generosity. Of course it was "only a dream." Still, as time has passed and I have continued to reflect on that dream, I have never lost my sense of gratitude to George for what I recognize now to be his essential goodwill and kindness. It is this, God's— and George's—gift of gratitude, that has increasingly enabled me to begin to make real progress with my temptations with respect to him, and to listen to him in meetings with actual kindness and even liking.

That is all the time we can spend in this letter thinking through the temptations that have their origins in us. At least this is true if we are to return to the question we have not yet answered, namely, if God does not deliberately lead us into temptation to test us or make us acknowledge God's power, as Joe did when he tempted Sally to take the drink, then what *can* Jesus be talking about when he teaches us to pray that God not "lead us into temptation, but deliver us from evil"? If God is not like Joe, then what *is* the God who might lead us into temptations like, and what kinds of temptations are they?

As I know from the difficulties I have already had in trying to think them through in order to write this letter, these questions are both important and hard to get hold of. If the questions are hard, however, I am finding it even harder to articulate what seem to me the only possible answers, but if you will bear with my stumblings and fumblings, because they are so crucial to who we are, I would like to try.

To talk about the nature of God's temptations, I believe, we need to begin with what 1 John 4 tells us about God and how God primarily relates to us. "God," says John, "is love" (1 John 4.8). As the writer of the epistle suggests, God loves us, the human beings God has created, so strongly, so deeply, so passionately, so absolutely, and so completely, that God's love can hardly even be described as a characteristic of God. When it comes to us, God *is* love.

A Place to Pray

Now, I realize, of course, that on the surface, there is nothing amazing in what I just said; after all, that God loves us—that God is love—is the first thing we learned in Sunday school. Yes, we learned it; this is true, but I am fairly sure neither of us was taught to think of God's love in the way John is thinking of it. I, at least, was told both that "God loves us in spite of who we are" and that "God has no need of us" too many times ever to have been able to believe that God would love anyone in the yearning manner in which scripture describes God's loving.

Many of the writers of the early church who are my teachers do not qualify God's love in this Sunday school way. The author of the Macarian Homilies, for example, describes God's responsive love as being like that of a mother so moved by her baby's crying that she cannot help picking the baby up to comfort it. Ephrem speaks of God's love in similar terms. They are not the only ones. Even Pseudo-Dionysius, the most austere and philosophical of the sixth-century theologians, describes the way as well as the reason God is intimately joined to all things, ourselves included, with these words:

> [God] in . . . his benign yearning for all is carried outside of himself in the loving care he has for everything. [God] is, as it were, beguiled by goodness, by love, and by yearning and is enticed away from his transcendent dwelling place and comes to abide within all things. . . . [6]

My friend, did you hear Pseudo-Dionysius's language? God is *"beguiled"* by love, God is *"enticed away* from [God's] eternal dwelling place" by love to dwell in all things, including us.

"Beguiled" and "enticed away" by love. Can you hear how radical these terms are? Far from loving us and the rest of creation at a calm, safe distance, in love God allows God's very self to be led by that which God loves into risky places. But certainly, this is the very fact the Incarnation of God made flesh among us affirms. God loved us enough to enter human life and become one of us, to participate in the lives we lead, not

---

6. The Divine Names IV, 13.

simply on God's immortal terms, but on our own vulnerable, suffering, mortal ones.

As for us, ours is a God who loves, and if we love this God who is love, we long to express that love by imitating God, that is, by loving those whom God loves in the way God loves, in an appropriately human manner. When we do love as God loves, we also sometimes find ourselves "beguiled" and "enticed" by love, or, as we might say, "tempted" by God's love to love beyond ourselves into the kinds of places of vulnerability, suffering, and danger into which God's love goes.

It is here, I think, at the point where we begin to imagine we might prefer to stop loving rather than endure the pain that loving carries with it, that we face the temptation that Jesus teaches us to pray to escape. We are tempted to betray love, to betray what we most love, and so to lose our very selves. This is the temptation into which we ask that God who is Love not lead us, and the evil from which we ask to be delivered.

Oh, my dear friend, how very hard this is, but from the time of Jesus and his prayer in the Garden of Gethsemane, I believe this is the way it has always been. This must surely be what Perpetua and the other martyrs of the early church knew as they found themselves tempted to turn their backs on their love of God and their Christian communities in order to spare their parents, protect their children, and save their own lives. It must have been what the old women I met in Russia knew as they prepared to throw their bodies in front of the moving tanks Stalin had ordered to raze their churches. The civil rights workers of the sixties when I was in seminary knew it, too.

Though I haven't experienced the same physical dangers, as a woman like many others who have helped open up the possibilities of younger women in a world that hasn't always wanted them, I've had to endure enough psychological suffering myself to want to turn and run, even if it meant betraying God's love, which had made me strong enough to do what I had already done. Believe me, it was once painful to go so against my family's expectations, as well as the expectations of the church and the educational communities to which I belonged. It hurt dreadfully to give up any claim I might have had to being a "nice" or "good" woman;

especially in my younger years, contempt was almost unbearable to me.

Do you think I prayed that God stop tempting me to give up by leading me into such hard places in the first place? I can assure you that I did. And do you imagine I asked God to rescue me from the sharp malice I suffered at the hands of those who didn't want to see women doing what I was trying to do, and the evil that would come to me interiorly if I gave up and refused to follow love? I did, indeed. If I were to be truthful with God, how could I help it?

I have had to pray this prayer in connection with Melissa, too. I remember so very clearly all that went through my mind that first week I learned about her cancer. I knew I had loved her for a long time; it was also true that I had never expected that my love would lead me to this place. One of my two basic fears is of loss and abandonment; the other is that when I am asked to do something important I won't be adequate to the task. If I were to try to enter into the experience of her cancer with Melissa and stay with her, I might very well be destroyed in the process. How could I stand it if I allowed myself to get even closer to her and then she died? What would happen if she needed me and I found myself leaving her because I wasn't strong enough to stay with her?

These fears were bad enough, and there were more. For my own mental and spiritual health, I have to write, but, as it is, I only have limited time to do it in the spaces around my teaching and speaking. If I were to be there for Melissa, I would have to decide to be willing to give up as much of this time as would be needed for the duration of her illness, whatever that duration might turn out to be.

I hated Melissa's having to be in the place into which her cancer was putting her, and I hated the thought of what might lie ahead of me, but, my friend, what could I do? It was love that had led me to where I was, love that had brought me into temptation. I knew it was only love and faithfulness to it that could deliver me from the evils that awaited me if I betrayed love.

So I decided I must recognize that there was no way I could tell Melissa, "I'm sorry, I can't be present to you and love you in your need because I have to have the time to write about the importance of love in human life." I also came to understand that, if I were to follow God who is Love, I would have to let myself be beguiled right past my fears of abandonment and inadequacy to go with love.

I find I still need to pray that God who is Love not lead me to places where I am inadequate to it, or where I will be abandoned in a way I cannot bear, and I continue to pray to be saved from the evil that would follow my own betrayals. And why, given what we have already said about the need to tell God what we actually feel, shouldn't I pray to be so rescued?

I find that I am being saved, too, though not in the way I meant when I originally prayed Jesus' prayer in this situation. For one, far from being swallowed up in my fears, from the very beginning, being with Melissa in her cancer has been an experience amazingly full of wonder, laughter, happiness, and holiness. It is a gift of love, God's and Melissa's, back to me. I am finding a little time to write, but I am not at all grieving the time I don't have. My fears are still there, but as I continue to look into myself to understand them and even to learn to accept them, they are losing their power over me.

Oddly enough, as the work of love goes on, I believe I am also discovering that, when it comes to distinguishing between the temptations God leads us into by love and the temptations we experience which come from within ourselves as we try to grow in love, there may not be as much difference as I once thought. In either case, it is Love that beguiles us out of ourselves to love, Love that entices us. In both cases, even when we pray to be rescued from the consequences of it, whatever its ultimate outcome, love is always a blessing.

At any rate, I thank you again, my dear friend, for your own love that is so sustaining to me now, as well as for the gift you offer of allowing me to write to you about these hard things. How would I ever find the blessing in them if we could not speak of them? God's love and my prayers be with you. You pray for me, too.

Roberta

CHAPTER SEVEN

My good friend,

We have come at last—or is it all at once?—to our reflections on "for yours is the kingdom and the power and the glory forever and ever." I ask you, so close to Christmas, how can I possibly write or even think about the early church's addition of such extravagant praise to the end of Jesus' prayer?

I am so busy, I hardly know what to do. I am still in a daze from the way Thanksgiving coincides with the end of the semester, and I am already grading take-home finals as I wait to give the exam in my big church history class. I have a major writing deadline at the end of the month, the first one ever I may not meet. Meanwhile, there are Christmas parties, Advent services, and end-of-the-year dinners. I have done almost none of my Christmas shopping. Will I get my presents in the mail on time this year for my out-of-town nearest and dearest? It makes my heart pound and my stomach churn just to think about it. Christmas cards are unwritten. The tree is up, at least, but the boxes for the ornaments are still sitting in the dining room, and I can't see the top of the buffet for the unanswered mail all over it.

As I look back, this has been such a year of ups and downs. Anxiously, Richard and I agreed that Benjamin could move back home from Chicago in January, and if that weren't traumatic enough, he moved out again and in with a friend six weeks later. We celebrated Mama's eightieth birthday with a surprise party in March at my brother Fred and my sister-in-law Linda's house in Louisville. At the beginning of April I learned of Melissa's cancer and she began her dreadful treatments. In May Richard quit teaching at Emory to become a full-time therapist. In the summer he went with me to a conference in England, never before having visited that place which has been an important part of my life for such a long time. From the end of August I taught and traveled and spoke and wrote until my eyeballs nearly rolled out on the floor. I am sure that one of my shoulders has been permanently lowered from the weight of carrying bags long distances through airports.

I am weary physically, emotionally, and spiritually, too. I haven't been eating right, and I can't get to my flute to practice. My prayer has been far more distracted than usual; though I know God is present to us no matter how disoriented and far we are from a sense of our own center, it has been tough to live off balance. I try to remind myself that it is simply the nature of human life to have periods of time like this. However chaotic it is now, I think about the almost daily chaos when the children were little and I wonder how I lived through it.

The time around Christmas has always been hard for me. As Martha would do, I worry that I won't get everything done, that papers will not be graded on time or that I will lose one, that people will not like their presents and so will be angry or feel rejected by me, that there will not be enough food for Christmas dinner, that the rolls will fall, or that the various dishes will not get done at the same time. Even without the stresses of the last few months, on the basis of how I generally used to be at this time of year, right now I would expect to feel at least helpless, discouraged, and depressed.

Yet, do you know, my friend, when I write about it now, I realize that though I am off balance, this year nothing really feels like a matter of life and death. I am tired, yes, but deep down I am also fairly sure everything will come out all right by the end of the month if I can only let things go a little, pace myself, and be observant of my real needs.

Busy or not, at the top of the list of my needs right now, I'll have to admit, is to ruminate with you on how I wish to pray the early church's doxology, "for yours is the kingdom, and the power, and the glory," which they added to Jesus' prayer. Indeed, I feel myself to be starving for such reflection precisely because of being so scattered.

I know where I need to begin, too. It is with the matter of praise. Praise to God. Easy enough to say; easy enough to command, for that matter. The psalms are full of it. "Praise befits the upright," says Psalm 33:1. "Sing praises to God, sing praises, for God is king over all the earth" (Psalm 47:6-7). "Praise him, praise him, all you little children," we sang when we were the little children. "Praise God from whom all blessings flow" we still sing in church, but what did we think praising God was about? What do we think we are saying?

As a little girl, at least, I surely couldn't imagine. How could a good God actually want praise and still be good unless there was something about God I didn't understand? Praise was a hard concept for me then, as I know it also was for you, as well as for a large number of people who grew up in this country about the same time we did. For us, it was a dubious enterprise to be on the receiving end of praise; we were taught to turn it down fearfully when it was offered to us, like candy from strangers. It was certainly not something we understood could ever legitimately be sought.

"How do I look?" I asked my mother, before a big birthday party when I was nine. She was fussing around in the small Pullman kitchen of our New York apartment, chopping some unrecognizable root vegetable for supper. I knew she cared about my appearance; she had already spent a considerable amount of time on it. That afternoon she had supervised a bath, rebraided my hair, and dressed me in a dark red velvet dress with a lace collar that she had been sewing for the big event throughout the preceding week or more. She had bought me fancy new shoes with straps. Of course, I would have preferred shoes without straps, like the big girls wore, but even with the baby shoes I was almost certain she would have to think I was splendid.

"How do I look?" I didn't just want her to think it; I wanted to hear her say it.

Almost shuddering, Mother glanced up at me and frowned. "Oh, you look all right," she answered, annoyed and disapproving. "Now, get your present, put on your coat, and go, or you'll be late for the party."

Utterly deflated and full of shame that I had not been able to keep myself from asking for praise when I knew it would get me in trouble, I put my arms in the heavy sleeves, buttoned myself up, and shuffled down the stairs.

"And don't forget to thank your hostess when you leave, young lady," Mama called out behind me as I pulled the door shut at the bottom.

My mother wasn't the only one in our garden apartments who would have reacted in this way to such a question from her or his child. Hardly any of our parents or teachers in those days of the forties believed in praising us. Sensible, loving adults didn't think that praise was good for children, even from grandparents. "Look how well she's doing that!" my Nanaw Cowan would say to my mother in front of me. Mama would look grim and reply, "Humph!"

I have very little idea what they believed was wrong with praising children. Mama, I know, was raised with plenty of praise. It probably had something to do with what the child-rearing experts said, or perhaps it was connected in their minds in some way with the Depression or with ideals of discipline and sacrifice the Second World War had imposed on everyone. I recall overhearing many conversations between my parents on the sources and dangers of "spoiling" children. Maybe they thought that if they praised us they would run the risk of giving us the bighead and making us brag; it might make us think we were somebody special, maybe even encourage us to talk back, or worse, make us disobedient. Then, again, maybe they were only training us to be adults who, like themselves, considered it both polite, modest, and, it seemed to me, moral always to turn away compliments in any form. It was certainly my mother's practice.

"You are such a good cook!" the dinner guest would say to her. "Your pie crust is just wonderful."

"It's so tough it's not fit to eat," she would always say in reply.

Though this problematic attitude toward praise was the general culture of the times, it certainly didn't make my cursory attempt to understand God's relationship to praise of God easy. Did God want to be praised? It would seem so from what I heard in Sunday school, but if God were good, how could that be?

As hard as all this was, however, my father brought me face to face with an even harder set of problems around the issue of praise—not of praise directed to God or toward me, but rather of praise and admiration that I might aim at other human beings. By conviction, in his younger years, my father never took the apparent goodness of any human being at face value. The son of a crime reporter, at one time or another for every major newspaper in Manhattan, he had been well trained in his father's professional cynicism. To my father, the better, the kinder, the more generous, the more honest someone looked or sounded, the more suspicious of that person he was. As he had heard from his own father, all politicians, philanthropists, priests, and their organizations were "on the take." He hated Eleanor Roosevelt and all other "do-gooders." Certainly, the motives of any teacher, Girl Scout leader, or other grown-up who wanted to spend time with children in his eyes were never pure almost by definition.

"Daddy, my teacher said she would stay after school to help Carol and me make blouses if we bring our own material," I remember telling him one night at supper time while we still lived in New York. I was so excited by visions of the beautiful clothing I was about to make and the time I was going to spend with the young teacher who liked me that I failed to notice the skeptical expression on his face. "She is so nice! She is so pretty and good to us! She never even yells at us." I wasn't cautious; I praised her openly.

Daddy glanced at me and grimaced, then sent a significant look in my mother's direction. "She's nice to you, is she?" he said. "Why is a grown woman staying after school with two little girls, I'd like to know? Your mother and I will talk about it later."

I groaned under my breath. I knew what he meant: he meant he wasn't going to let me stay after school and sew. "But Daddy," I began again, "she is so..."

"No arguing, young lady, do you understand?" he interrupted.

I didn't dare say anything good to him about my teacher for a long time after that. Rather, part of me wondered myself what my father was hinting was wrong with my teacher that she would want to spend time with me, and what was wrong with me that I couldn't see what was the matter with my teacher.

When I was a child it was hard having the adults I admired, some of whom were good to me, so systematically discredited. It was painful, to say the least, to know that my father believed I ought never to give my heart completely to any grown-up on the unapproved list because they, their accomplishments, and even their love were never to be trusted. Wanting to admire and to praise but being taught that I ought not to do it even in my deepest self divided me against myself. It made me think there was something wrong with me for loving and being loved by such unworthy people. It paralyzed me with guilt and longing, and it opened up in me a loneliness, a great emptiness that I did not know how to fill.

My friend, for most of my life I have not known how to receive praise. It has not only embarrassed me, at some nonrational level I have actually felt that the fact that it was aimed at me in the first place was the sign that whatever I had done that provoked it must have been in some way wrong. Though I will try to tell you in a little while how that has begun to change, let me say this for now: I am very glad that over the last thirty or forty years our culture has come to reverse itself over the matter of children receiving praise. Though I think we sometimes go overboard with it now, and that causes its own problems, we finally seem to be acknowledging how important recognition is to everyone's well-being.

At the same time, it scares me nearly witless to think that almost everybody today seems to share to one degree or another in the kind of cynicism my father embraced as a young man. (Thank God, he was beautifully cured of it before he died!) Everyone suspects the worst of public figures whether they be in sports, the arts, or business. Hardly anybody believes the speeches politicians make, and the papers are full of the reports of awful abuse that is taking place in our churches at this

A Place to Pray

very moment. The papers play subtly on our fears of meeting destruction at the hands of neighbors who are not what they seem to be, of teenagers, of "welfare-cheaters," of relatives, of "criminals," of people of different religious or political persuasions than ours, of "illegal aliens." We eat it all up, and our children are often as cynical and untrusting as we are.

Whatever are we to do? Certainly, the world is full of dangerous and untruthful people who, in the guise of good, prey on other people, but, my friend, our cynical mistrust of the appearance of goodness and even innocence is serious. As Christians, do we really want to go through life waiting for others to "show their true colors," which we always expect to be ugly? Do we actually want to believe that, however God feels about us, at core human beings are truly rotten? Do we want to decide that the praise and admiration we would direct toward others is never justified but is the activity of fools?

I won't and oughtn't to believe it if I want to affirm the love of God, the goodness of the whole of creation God has made, and the reality of our own human making in the Image of God.

If we take the psalms seriously, we have to wonder whether praise of God, at least, is not the essential activity of all that is. As we hear of them in Psalm 19, it certainly seems to be the case for stars and the sky and even night and day.

> The heavens are telling the glory of God;
>> and the firmament proclaims [God's] handiwork.
> Day to day pours forth speech,
>> and night to night declares knowledge.
> There is no speech, nor are there words;
>> their voice is not heard;
> yet their voice goes out through all the earth.

Praise, the ability to receive it, but even more, the capacity to give it, is absolutely necessary to human life. Do you remember the lines from the first paragraph of Augustine's great prayer of praise, his spiritual auto-biography which we know as the *Confessions*?

> [Humanity], he says, is one of your creatures, Lord, and [our] instinct is to praise you .... The thought of you stirs [us] so deeply that [we] cannot be content unless we praise you, because you made us for yourself and our hearts find no peace until they rest in you.[1]

As I read Augustine, praising God isn't just something we *do,* an activity we engage in among other activities. It is a fundamental *way of being* toward God, an attitude of heart toward deepest reality without which we cannot even rest within the space of our own lives.

This kind of praise of God is the opposite of cynicism. It is the disposition of the foreign Magi who, following one of those praising stars we just heard about in Psalm 19, came from the East to bring presents to the new king of the Jews. Not suspicious of the family's apparent lack of social status, these same Magi, scripture tells us, were "filled with joy" when the star that guided them stopped above the house where Mary and the baby were. Without any qualm reported in the Bible, they left their costly gifts of gold, frankincense, and myrrh and went home happy.

Praise is the song of the angels who summoned the shepherds to the City of David in the middle of the night to see the baby Messiah, the one who was lying, not in a golden cradle in the temple or a palace, but in a shed for animals, in the food trough of donkeys. It is the shepherd's song, too, as they returned "glorifying and praising God" to the same cold fields they had earlier left.

The birth of Jesus was a happy event, but the kind of deep praise we are talking about here does not depend upon things going well. It is as the prophet Habakkuk says:

---

1. Augustine, *Confessions,* 1.1.1., R. S. Pine-Coffin, trans. (Baltimore: Penguin Books, 1961), p. 21.

A Place to Pray

Though the fig tree does not blossom,
and no fruit is on the vines;
though the produce of the olive fails,
and the fields yield no food;
though the flock is cut off from the fold,
and there is no herd in the stalls,
yet I will rejoice in the LORD;
I will exult in the God of my salvation.
GOD, the Lord, is my strength;
he makes my feet like the feet of a deer;
and makes me tread upon the heights.
(Habakkuk 3:17-19)

Where there is love in a marriage, it is for richer or poorer, for better or for worse. It does not cease with the loss of a job, a failure in the crops, a serious illness, or even the senility of one of the partners. Neither does its close relative, praise.

Praise. I ask God for the gift of praise, because I have come to believe that it is one of the most basic of the dispositions, perhaps even the most basic, of the soul of the one who would love—surely our aim and end, as you and I have been saying in our previous letters. I am certain that it is very close to the fundamental virtue of humility which the Desert Abbas and Ammas teach. To praise is to abandon my need to prove myself by being superior to others. The praise of God and the praise of God's images is the opposite of the sort of pride which is always measuring itself against the accomplishments and failures of the ones around me. It is the opposite of shame. Surely, to praise is to recognize God's generous love for all of God's creatures over which sunlight is equally shed, whether or not we human beings consider them worthy.

To praise God and to praise others is to know and to rejoice in the fact that everything of value I do as a human being, even when I pray, I do only because I have been enabled and empowered by God or by God's human images. It is to celebrate, rather than resent, the fact that I cannot create my own life by my accomplishments or my possessions, for everything I have, I have received as gifts—from my parents, my husband, and my children; from the generosity of the British system of education in the sixties, the school where I teach, and my students; from the folk with whom I worship and the saints who preserved the *Sayings of the Fathers;* from the makers of my computer to the editor of my books. My life depends upon what others, even my enemies, have given me. "Why are you fighting?" Dorotheos asks his embattled monks. "Don't you know you should be praying, 'by the prayers of my brother, save me?'"

The disposition to praise is the very opposite of restless acquisitiveness and the need to control, even in circumstances where such a need would seem perfectly reasonable. Though he doesn't call it praise, my dear sixth-century teacher Dorotheos of Gaza speaks of something similar, which was known in the ancient monastic tradition as "freedom from the passions." This freedom comes from learning to cut off "extraneous desires," and those who are able to learn it "find [themselves] always doing what [they want] to do. For not having [their] own special fancies, [they fancy] every single thing that happens to [them]."[2] Such a cutting off of desire, such a praise, such an appreciation for what is, is what Melissa has shown me as she has gone through her treatment for cancer.

"Roberta," she said to me that first day we had lunch together after her diagnosis, "I am striking the word 'success' from my vocabulary right now. I have known so many sick people who were so focused on going all over the world to find a cure for their disease that they could not appreciate and be present to the life they had. Instead, they died full only of a sense of failure."

I remember pondering the application of her words to me. It seems to me that such a capacity for praise comes in on the wings of holy vulnerability. It is surely what we would expect right now as we wait for God once more to come among us as a helpless, trusting, laughing baby who would put its fingers in the mouth of every stranger who approaches it with a smile. It is certainly what I have continued to learn these last few months as I have watched Melissa after the worst of her treatments lying

---

2. "On Renunciation," p. 89.

on her back porch petting Miouwser, her tiger cat, on her lap as she listens with total, happy concentration to the birds' songs outside. I can see for myself that such an appreciation of the goodness of life is the very opposite of the fear of death.

I think of an English friend of mine, a clergyperson who, when he walks down the street, stops, speaks, and puts a coin in the hand of every beggar who asks for it without worrying whether he will be proved to have been made a fool of if he learns later that the beggar is a fraud. Praise opens us directly to reality, to one another, and to God. Praise draws us close to one another and teaches us that we are not alone at the very same moment that it fills us with awe at one another's, and God's, absolute, mysterious otherness.

Praise as a disposition sees with a single eye. It is not divided against itself, one half speaking "she has done well," the other half whispering "but not as well as it's possible to do." Nor does it try to say, "I love God," or even "I meet God in creation," while it waits with a knowing, superior smile on its face for the base, the corrupt, or the selfish to show itself in God's images.

Indeed—and I think this is the most important thing I have learned this year—praise understands, believes in, and waits for the fundamental goodness that lies at the heart of all things that reflect the being of God, especially when it is to be found in other people, the images of God.

So many times over the past few months have I wondered at the stories Melissa has told me. Did you know, when they heard she was suffering with cancer, some of the very folks she once found so difficult to work with brought her flowers, left her encouraging messages, and sent her books. Elderly neighbors she has hardly known have carried in to her and her family wonderful home-cooked meals, desserts included; I have eaten some of them myself. And people I have met on trips, strangers to me and, even more, strangers to her, have mailed her, and me too, cards, letters, and even gifts. My friend, having seen all this gratuitous human love, I would have to choose, now, not to see it everywhere. What unexpected generosity, kindness, and faithfulness even strangers show to one another every day! How can I think of writing off all that goodness as irrelevant to each person as he or she "really is" in the face of all that good? How are we really? Flawed and damaged, yes, vulnerable and mortal, but at bottom the images of God, even of the generous love of God.

It is the awareness of this human-divine generosity, this reaching out in love, more than any other, I think, that has helped me at last begin to learn not only how to praise but how to receive praise in the form of compliments from other people for what it is.

A woman arranges to speak with me privately the next day after a talk I have given on the way our relationships with God are shaped by our earlier relationships with our parents. There are tired lines around her eyes, but her mouth is smiling.

"Oh," she says. "What you said yesterday was the most helpful thing I ever heard. I spent five years in therapy and couldn't get as far as I got last night when I stayed up thinking about it."

Impulsively, she throws her arms around me and hugs me, then draws away to look me earnestly in the face. "I know you must be a lifesaver to a lot of people," she says.

"No, no." Distressed, I begin to answer her. This is bad for her to say and for me to listen to. Then, all at once, I really hear what she is trying to convey to me, and it has nothing to do with my goodness or badness, my insights or my abilities to articulate something difficult. It is not *about* me and what I have done at all: it is *to* me, and it is a *gift*.

"Your words have helped me, and I am grateful," she is telling me. "In gratitude, I offer you some of the love that has been called out of me, and I ask you to accept it in the form of praise. May it feed you, sustain you, and delight you in return."

"I'm so glad you found what I said helpful," I respond to her. I receive her gift, and I do feel fed, sustained, and delighted by her and by God. "Thank you so very much."

Out of this I have come to understand, as I could not as a child, not only why good people accept praise, but why God wants praise from us. Praise links us to God in love. The praise of the psalmist is an expression of

A Place to Pray

delight, and so is our own praise. Of course God wants it. It is the recognition, both conscious and unconscious, that God's name is hallowed in all things. It is a reaching out of the heart with thanksgiving to green eyes, to the curve of a mouth, to the feel of cat fur against skin. It is taking pleasure in a bar of Mozart, in the shape of a mountain, in a fuzzy head made bald by chemotherapy, in a baby's fat arms, in the structure of a sentence. It is wondering at the alienness of a red-tailed hawk staring back from a fence post, at light shimmering on wet leaves, at the distance of a constellation, at the ethereal translucence of a white moon-jelly in an aquarium.

Yet praise is sorrow, too, a sorrow of recognition for the suffering of those God loves. It is grief for the parents of a young woman who contracted an improbably rare disease at work and died, for another woman who cannot make enough money to pay her bills and support her children, for a widower who has never made friends on his own and doesn't know what to do now that his wife is dead, for a child who is just funny-looking enough that the other children at school treat her with contempt, for a homeless man who cannot stay in a shelter because "they" will get him indoors, for the possible death of Melissa from cancer. It is weeping for the babies everywhere slaughtered like the innocents to protect the thrones of the Herods of our world; for the children murdered in war, worn out in factories, bewildered in the streets. It is grieving for the lost green places of the soul where grass once grew, for houses burned down or never built, for parched throats, for stinking sores, and for lonely eyes. It is sorrow for dreams drifted away, hearts hurt. It is sadness for the dissonance we all must finally feel between the way things are in this life, and the good we know God wants for us.

My friend, praise *is* saying "yes" to God in spite of everything that is truly wounded. It is a great "yes" for all that is, for all that has been, and for all that is to come. It is "yes" to the kingdom that was God's in our beginnings, from the ancient nothing of primeval chaos to the making of ourselves in God's image. God's is the kingdom of our history, of the holy lives of our distant ancestors of other races, nations, and tongues on other continents; of the equally holy lives of our mothers and fathers in the faith—Abraham, David, Miriam, Ruth, Elizabeth and Mary the second Miriam, Anthony, Poemen, Gertrude, Julian, and so many others we will never know; of our great-grandparents, our grandparents, our parents, and even of ourselves.

It is "yes" to the present kingdom, which is also God's, in spite of its sorrows, its sins and deaths. It is "yes" to innocence, to goodness, to kindness, and to beauty, which are everywhere hidden around us; "yes" to the people of God who yearn for God and love God and one another as best they can. It is "yes" to the simplicities and the complexities of the kingdom, its hiddenness and its openness, and all its partial healings.

It is "yes" to God's partially present and still future kingdom for which we daily pray "your kingdom come, your will be done," the kingdom in which all shall be healed, all set right, all made well, the yet unknown kingdom of love over which the Lamb shall reign.

It is "yes" to the impossible power of God which is love so improbable that we see it best in the person of God among us as a tiny baby in Bethlehem lying in a feed trough, and "yes" to the equally improbable glory of God shining over the heads of shepherds, over slums, over sickrooms, over a man in prison, over another man on a cross.

My friend, every "yes" is praise, and so I pray to our God this Advent for the gift of it with the expectation that I will not be given a stone instead: "Our God, today let me add my prayer of praise to all those who have belonged to you, who belong to you now, and who will ever belong to you, for yours is the kingdom and the power and the glory forever. Amen!"

Enough for now. I am off to my work, which at the moment is practicing my poor, neglected flute for the Advent service at Elaine and Dale's tomorrow morning. Blessings on you, my good and faithful companion. I thank you with my whole heart for being the occasion of these reflections on Jesus' prayer these last few months.

May the blessings of the Christ Child rest happily on you, and may you find a place to pray everywhere you go. My love as always,

Roberta